TH
4816
.B525
1988

Bianchina, Paul.

Kitchen remodeling

$23.95

DATE			

KITCHEN REMODELING
A DO-IT-YOURSELFER'S GUIDE

For Rose
The beautiful push I need to keep going

No. 3011
$23.95

KITCHEN REMODELING
A DO-IT-YOURSELFER'S GUIDE
PAUL BIANCHINA

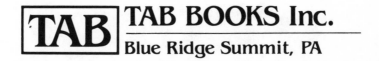

TAB BOOKS Inc.
Blue Ridge Summit, PA

FIRST EDITION
FIRST PRINTING

Copyright © 1988 by TAB BOOKS Inc.
Printed in the United States of America

Library of Congress Cataloging in Publication Data

Bianchina, Paul.
Kitchen remodeling : a do-it-yourselfer's guide / by Paul
Bianchina.
p.   cm.
Includes index.

ISBN 0-8306-9011-5   ISBM 0-8306-9311-4 (pbk.)
1. Kitchens—Remodeling—Amateurs' manuals. I. Title.
TH4816.B525   1988
643′.3—dc19   88-22729
                                                              CIP

TAB BOOKS Inc. offers software for
sale. For information and a catalog,
please contact TAB Software Department,
Blue Ridge Summit, PA 17294-0850.

Questions regarding the content of this book
should be addressed to:

Reader Inquiry Branch
TAB BOOKS Inc.
Blue Ridge Summit, PA 17294-0214

Cover photograph courtesy of Merillat Industries, Inc.

Contents

Acknowledgments

I would like to extend my deep appreciation to all of the following individuals and companies whose input and assistance helped tremendously in the creation of this book. In particular, I would like to thank Rose Bianchina for her editing and her constant encouragement; Chas, Annette, and Chris at Kitchen Concepts for letting me pester them; John and Ruth for the use of their kitchen; Mike O'Brien of Western Wood Products Association for his pictures and his sunny disposition; Helen L. Cross of The American Home Lighting Institute for her help; Jean Francis of American Olean Tile for all the great pictures; and Kim Baxley of McKone & Company for the wonderful volume of material on Wilsonart.

American Home Lighting Institute
American Olean Tile
American Plywood Association
American Standard
Amerock Corporation
Cheever, Ellen, CKD, ASID
Congoleum Corporation
Diamond Cabinets
E.I. du Pont de Nemours Company, Inc.
General Electric Company
John and Ruth
Kitchen Concepts
Kitchen Kompact, Inc.
Lightolier
Manina, Steve
Medallion Kitchens of Minnesota
Merillat Industries, Inc.
Merrit Industries
Moen, a Division of Stanadyne
Nutone Products
Ralph Wilson Plastics Company
Resilient Floor Covering Institute
Scheirich Cabinetry
Supanich, Mic, M.J.S. Construction
Wallcovering Information Bureau
Western Wood Products Association
Wood Moulding and Millwork Producers

Introduction

Welcome to today's kitchen!

No longer is the kitchen a utilitarian center, a dull and drab place of drudgery hidden away in a corner, a room just big enough for the basics of meal preparation. The kitchen of today is bright and cheerful, with hanging plants and room to move. State-of-the-art appliances sparkle against the rich tones of natural wood cabinets. Storage space abounds, and convenience is the key word.

From quaint Colonial styling to sleek European cabinetry, today's kitchen reflects who you are. It makes a statement about your lifestyle, and proudly holds a central place in the household activities.

Today's kitchen is much more than a place to only make a meal. It's a 24-hour cafeteria for the entire family, for everything from a solitary breakfast to a seven-course dinner. It's a meeting place, a gathering spot for friends and neighbors. It's a home office, complete with a computer. It's an extension of the family room, with a microwave oven for quick snacks and a built-in television. It's a meal-planning center, with cookbooks proudly displayed. It's all these things and more—it's whatever you want it to be.

That's the purpose of *Kitchen Remodeling— A Do-It-Yourselfer's Guide*. It's complete—from planning through the often overlooked task of removing the old kitchen; from wiring and plumbing to fun accessories. *Kitchen Remodeling—A Do-It-Yourselfer's Guide* is much more than just an idea book, although it's certainly that. It's a real-world guide to the pleasures and problems of remodeling the most important room in the house. This book will take your ideas and show you how to turn them into the reality of the kitchen you've always dreamed of!

Chapter 1

The Preliminaries

THERE IS NO DOUBT THAT IN TODAY'S HOME, THE kitchen is the center of all activity. Kitchen remodeling, more than any other home project you'll undertake, is a tremendous responsibility. It should be undertaken slowly, with care and thought, to have the best chances of successful completion. Every member of the family should be given a chance for their input, and all the ideas should be carefully considered and discussed before a final plan is worked out.

The purpose of this chapter is to introduce you to some of the practical considerations of kitchen remodeling. Becoming well informed about what's ahead—the joys and the headaches, the pleasures and the problems—can go a long way toward achieving the kitchen of your dreams.

The kitchen is, typically, the most expensive room in the house to remodel (Fig. 1-1). Cabinetry, appliances, counters, a large amount of plumbing and electrical wiring—all these things add up when concentrated in one room. A well-designed and well-constructed kitchen is the showplace of the home, combining efficient practicality with an eye-pleasing decor.

For many people, designing a new or remodeled kitchen is a job best left to the professional, and this is the first choice you'll need to make.

CHOOSING A DESIGNER

If you are considering using a designer for your kitchen, the effort you put into finding the right one for you will pay off over and over. The right designer should guide you through the hundreds of decisions involved in kitchen remodeling, blending your tastes and desires into a practical, workable room that really expresses you, while staying within your budget!

The first way to look for a designer is by soliciting recommendations from others. Proud owners of new kitchens speak highly of a designer's abilities. If you know of anyone who's just had his kitchen remodeled, even a friend of a friend of a friend, give him a call. Ask who the designer was, and if the person was satisfied with the job.

If you don't know of anyone who's just had kitchen work done, the next place to try would be local kitchen and bath centers. Check the Yellow Pages under "kitchen." These centers, which specialize in design, sales, and installation, usually have highly qualified designers on staff. Some smaller kitchen centers might work with independent, free-lance designers and can make recommendations.

Other possibilities in your initial hunt for a designer might be retail outlets, such as those selling cabinets, appliances, or interior accessories. You

1

might also check the Yellow Pages under "Interior Designers," "Interior Decorators," "Designers," or "Architects." Any of these sources might have staff kitchen designers, or be able to steer you in the right direction.

When you have the names of some designers, give them a call and set up an appointment with each for a preliminary meeting. This meeting should be no more than a brief get together to see the designer's shop and displays, if the person has one, and to have the opportunity to meet and see how you like the person. A good rapport with your designer is essential, and this meeting will give you the opportunity to see if you think you can work well together.

One thing you'll want to learn at this preliminary meeting is the designer's fee. Some designers work on a flat fee for the entire kitchen, while some work by the hour. If the designer is affiliated with a kitchen and bath center or other retailer, all or part of the fee is often waived if you purchase a certain amount of goods from the store, and this can present a real money-saving opportunity.

However the fees are handled, knowing about them up front will save any possible misunderstandings and hard feelings later. You'll know what to expect so you can budget for them without any surprises.

If the first meeting goes well and you think you'd like to work with this designer, ask for the names of some recent clients, and request to contact them. This is a very common request, and one that the designer should be ready, and willing, to agree to. If he doesn't, consider looking elsewhere.

Before your next meeting with the designer, do your homework. Call some of the clients from the list you were given, explain that you're shopping for a designer, and see if you might ask them some

Fig. 1-1. A beautifully remodeled kitchen, with all its cabinetry, appliances, and plumbing, requires a well thought out plan (Courtesy of Kitchen Kompact).

questions. Among the things you might want to ask are:

- [ ] Did the designer let the homeowner's ideas come out, or did he try to push his own ideas?
- [ ] Was he cooperative and easy to work with during any changes that came up (and there will be changes!)?
- [ ] Was he competent and well-informed, both from a practical, "hammer and nails" aspect and from an artistic standpoint?
- [ ] Did he have access to a full line of cabinets, appliances, accessories, floor and wall coverings, countertops, etc.?
- [ ] Did he provide sufficient drawings during the design stage to allow thorough visualization of the completed kitchen?
- [ ] Did he help the homeowner stay within a predetermined budget?
- [ ] Does it "work," now that the accessories have been in the kitchen for a while? Is the layout good? Were the cabinets, appliances, and accessories well chosen?
- [ ] Did he complete the project on time?
- [ ] Were any installers or subcontractors the designer supplied (or recommended) competent and cooperative? How were the finished products?
- [ ] Above all, would the homeowner recommend the designer to others?

If the person you're talking with is cooperative, ask if you could stop by for a visit. Most satisfied clients are delighted to show off their new kitchen. This visit will give you a good opportunity to see the designer's and the installer's work, and perhaps even gather some new ideas for your own kitchen.

DECIDING WHAT YOU WANT

When you're comfortable with a particular designer, both from your meeting with him and from client recommendations, make an appointment to begin the preliminary design work. This second meeting should be at your home so that the designer can see your home and existing kitchen, and meet your family.

Your designer will need to ask you a number of questions to help him to evaluate your needs. Some designers use an actual questionnaire that they'll have you fill out in advance. With or without the questionnaire, before your second meeting you should have taken the time to ask yourself some of the following questions.

Evaluating What's Existing

The best place to begin deciding what you want out of your new kitchen is by taking a good close look at your existing kitchen. Take a sheet of paper, divide it into two columns, and label one column "Like" and the other column "Dislike." With the help of other family members, list every feature about the kitchen, no matter how small or insignificant, that you like and don't like. You might want to actually sit in the kitchen while you make your list.

If you're like most people, your "Dislike" list will be considerably longer than your "Like" list, but it's equally important to focus on those items you like about your existing kitchen. A certain set of cabinets, the height of an appliance, the size of a sunny window—if these are things you like in the old kitchen that you want to incorporate in the new one, they're worth listing.

Obviously, certain things will be of greater importance than others when you make your list, but be as thorough as possible. For example, the kitchen's biggest drawback may be that it's entirely too small, and this is at the top of your "Dislike" list. Also list things like too dark, drab decor, too much traffic, no place for a guest to sit, too cold, sink's too small, and anything else that bothers you.

Evaluating Yourself

A key element in designing a kitchen that really suits you and your family is to look at your lifestyle, and this is something your designer probably will want to discuss with you also. As you sift through the information and ask yourself the following questions, be as honest with yourself as possible.

With the kitchen as the acknowledged focal point of the house, both from a social and entertaining standpoint and from the standpoint of day-to-day activities, understanding how you use it is important.

Consider the following questions, and list your answers and comments on another sheet of paper:

- [ ] How many people are there in your family?
- [ ] Are you expecting any changes in that number in the near future (teenager leaving home, new baby due, family members coming home to stay for an extended period, etc.)? Upcoming changes are important to plan for in sizing your new kitchen.
- [ ] Is the current size of the kitchen roughly adequate for your family's needs? Your honest answer to this question is important in determining if more space is needed in the new kitchen, and how much more. It eventually will aid you in deciding if you will just need more cabinet space within the existing room, or if you actually require more square footage.
- [ ] How many people in the house actually work in the kitchen? List each person by name, and note the approximate number of hours each one spends in the kitchen every day.
- [ ] Are there occasions when two people work in the kitchen at the same time? If so, how often does this occur? If it's a regular occurrence (happens several times a week), you might want to plan for a two-cook kitchen.
- [ ] Will the new kitchen require any special features, such as for someone who's disabled, or for someone who's shorter than average?
- [ ] Are meal times usually consistent, or does your house sometimes resemble a 24-hour cafeteria? Look at this question closely. It will help you determine if you need a large area for a formal dining table, or if a small serving bar in the kitchen might be more appropriate. Quite often, a large, unused formal dining room can be opened up to provide a larger kitchen.
- [ ] Do you normally prepare formal meals for the whole family, or lighter, more informal meals for certain members at certain times? This question will help you decide on how much counter space you'll need, what types of appliances you might need (a microwave might be essential, for example), and what seating arrangements might be most appropriate.

- [ ] Is the kitchen a gathering place for friends and relatives, even when you're not actually entertaining? If yes, do you like it that way? Some people don't like others congregating in the kitchen, so limiting the size and seating or providing a way of closing the kitchen off from other rooms might be just the thing for you. If the answer's no, do you want it to be a gathering place? With today's more informal lifestyles, you might wish the kitchen was open to the rest of the house, with seating at one of the counters for guests.
- [ ] How often do you entertain, and in what manner? Again, this is an important question. Do you have large, formal dinner parties requiring extra seating space or perhaps a second oven? Is your entertaining mostly informal, centered around an outdoor pool or patio? A serving window to the outside might be just the thing for handling guests by the pool, while saving time and steps.
- [ ] Are the current traffic patterns a problem? How would you change them? This two-part question might be something that you found the answers to while answering some of the other questions. Traffic patterns usually emerge as a result of kitchen layout and door placement, and they're not always ideal. You might want to start thinking about closing off doorways or opening up another access to the patio.
- [ ] Do you perform any special, kitchen-related activities, such as baking or candy making? You might wish to incorporate space for a separate baking center with bulk dispensers for flour and other ingredients, or perhaps an area with a special marble countertop for candy. Maybe large storage bins for use while canning is important, or a big, sunny window shelf for growing fresh herbs.
- [ ] Do you need a work area in the kitchen for non-cooking activities, such as planning meals and preparing a grocery list, or even paying bills? If you do, now's the time to plan for it.

The Last List

By now you should have accumulated a fair-sized list of likes, dislikes, and answers. To be sure you're ready for the designer or to help focus your thoughts and ideas if you're doing your own designing, you'll want to make one more list. This final list will have three columns: "Must Have," "Would Like If Possible," and "Nice, But Could Do Without."

In the first column, put those things that your new kitchen absolutely must have. For example, this list might include more counter space, microwave, pantry, or even little things like spice rack and roll-out shelves. If it's something you really don't want to do without, list it here.

Column two should include those items that you'd like to incorporate into the kitchen if it's physically and financially possible. This might include hardwood floor, triple-compartment sink, six-burner cooktop, or new refrigerator.

Finally, column three might be no more than daydreams that you saw in a magazine, such as a dumbwaiter for the downstairs, or an open barbecue.

What is a nonessential daydream to you might be a necessity to someone else, and everyone's list will be different. The point is to be as honest with yourself as possible. Don't insist on adding an expensive appliance you'll hardly ever use if you really can't afford it. On the other hand, don't be afraid to list something in the "Must Have" column that might seem a little extravagant to someone else if you really want it, even if it stretches your budget. Most people only remodel their kitchen once, and you want to be sure to get what you want!

All of these exercises are designed to help you decide what you really want and need in your new kitchen, and they're important. Focusing your thoughts in this manner prepares you for dealing with the designer, and it goes a long way toward getting you the kitchen you've dreamed of at a price you can afford.

CONTRACTORS VS. DO-IT-YOURSELF

Kitchen remodeling is not the overwhelming task it once was. Modular cabinets, preformed counter-tops, and plumbing and electrical components designed for the do-it-yourselfer all have combined to make things easier, within reason. As you did with your preliminary lists, you need to ascertain how much you're comfortable with undertaking.

Be honest with yourself about your abilities. If you've never done any major remodeling, you might want to leave the entire project in the hands of a contractor. This decision will ensure that the job is done quickly and professionally, and with a guarantee against future problems. Another alternative is to subcontract those skills you aren't familiar with, such as plumbing or electrical wiring, and concentrate your efforts on tear-out, drywall, painting, or other areas you're comfortable with.

Time is another important factor to consider. Living in a home without a kitchen quickly tries the patience of the entire family. If you don't have the time to finish the project quickly, leave the bulk of the work to a contractor.

Choosing a Contractor

If you're working with a designer, chances are there is one or more qualified contractors that the designer has worked with in the past. This is a good place to start. Because the designer's reputation is on the line, any contractor he recommends is usually competent and competitively priced. Again, try to talk with someone who has used the contractor in the past, and get a personal recommendation. Also, try to see an example of the contractor's work.

It's usually best to get at least two bids on the work. Compare them carefully to be certain both contractors are bidding the same items (both labor and quality of materials), then choose the one you feel will do the best job for you. Remember that the lowest bidder is not always the best choice. Select a contractor you think you can work with and whose abilities you have faith in.

You should have a contract with the contractor that spells out all the work to be done, the agreed-on price, and any schedule of payments. Read and understand the contract completely before signing it, and don't sign it if it contains blank spaces.

BUILDING PERMITS

Whether or not your job requires a building permit depends on the scope of the project and local regulations. Painting, redecorating, or just replacing cabinets usually do not require a permit. Structural changes or changes in the plumbing or wiring usually do. If in doubt, check with your designer or contractor, or call your local building department and describe the job.

If a permit is required, decide who will obtain it—you, the contractor, or the designer—and also who will pay for it. The permit will add slightly to the cost of the job, but it will ensure that the work is being done correctly and safely.

Chapter 2

Planning and Design

EVERY SUCCESSFUL REMODELING PROJECT BEGINS at the beginning—with a solid, workable, well-thought-out plan. Nowhere is this more true than in the kitchen. As mentioned in Chapter 1, the kitchen is the most expensive room in the house to remodel, with virtually every square inch crammed with costly cabinets, appliances, wiring, and plumbing. This expense makes a comprehensive plan all the more important, and it's something that can't be stressed enough.

If you're dealing with a designer, much of the design and planning work will be done for you. You still must be an active participant in the planning, however; so a working knowledge of the design and planning principle in this chapter will be very helpful. If you're doing your own designing, these principles are essential.

THE PRINCIPAL WORK CENTERS

The first step in designing a kitchen is to understand that it is not just one big room, but rather a combination of smaller, separate work centers. Each work center has a specific purpose. It is the relationship between these areas within the kitchen that makes an efficient, or inefficient, design.

Take a moment to study each work center, and then relate them to your existing kitchen. This study will help you understand what comprises each area and how the relationships come into play. It also might help you to see what's inefficient about your existing kitchen, and how you can overcome those problems with the new design.

The Refrigerator/Food Storage Center

The first of the three work centers is the refrigerator/food storage center. The focal point of this area is, of course, the refrigerator, but it also encompasses pantry and cabinet space for non-refrigerated foods. Quite often, storage also will be provided within this area for freezer wrap, storage containers, etc. In most kitchens, only the refrigerator/freezer is placed in this area. Full-sized freezers for bulk storage of frozen foods are placed elsewhere, usually outside the kitchen itself.

When planning the location of the refrigerator center, try to locate it near the area where food will be prepared to minimize the walking distance. If possible, also locate it near the doorway through which you will be bringing the groceries. Do not place the refrigerator next to the oven because the oven's

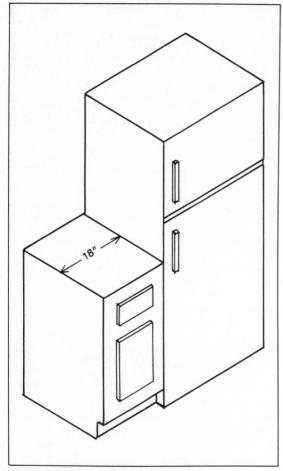

Fig. 2-1. Provide 18 inches of counterspace on the latch side of the refrigerator.

however, the oven is usually located near the cooktop.

Storage is provided in this area for pots, pans, and other cooking utensils, and also for seasonings, spices, oil, and other items frequently used while cooking. A range hood, if used, also would be part of this area.

You'll need to provide a minimum of 24 inches of counter space on one side of the cooktop (Fig. 2-2), preferably on both sides. This counter space is essential for serving foods prepared on the cooktop. If possible, the counter should be heatproof or have a heatproof insert where hot pots can be placed.

A separate oven (Fig. 2-3), needs to have at least 18 inches of space next to it. If the oven is located some distance from the cooktop, this will have to be a separate base cabinet and counter. If the oven is adjacent to the cooktop, it can share counter space.

The Cleanup Center

The sink is the focal point of the third principal work area: the cleanup center (Fig. 2-4). It is here that food is washed and prepared, and cleanup is performed. Within the cleanup center is also the garbage disposal, the dishwasher, and, if used, the trash compactor.

A dishwasher is usually placed to the left of the sink for easiest filling by a right-handed person. If you are not installing a dishwasher now but are considering adding one later, install a separate 24-inch cabinet next to the sink. It can easily be removed later, leaving the appropriate space for the dishwasher.

Storage is provided at the cleanup center for soap, dish towels, and the like. Knives, brushes, and other items for trimming and washing food should be nearby. Cabinets for dishes, glasses, and flatware are usually nearby also. Counters of at least 30 inches should be placed on both sides of the sink to efficiently handle dirty dishes.

The Preparation Center

There is a fourth key in the basic kitchen layout: the preparation center. In smaller kitchens, the

heat can adversely affect the operation of the refrigerator.

A minimum of 18 inches of counter space (Fig. 2-1), should be provided next to the refrigerator, on the latch side. This gives you a place to set food that is being taken out of or put into the refrigerator.

The Cooking/Serving Center

The cooking/serving center is the second work area you need to be concerned with. It consists of the range or, if the cooktop and oven are separate units, the cooktop. A separate oven can be placed virtually anywhere in the kitchen, and does not constitute a work area in its own right. For convenience,

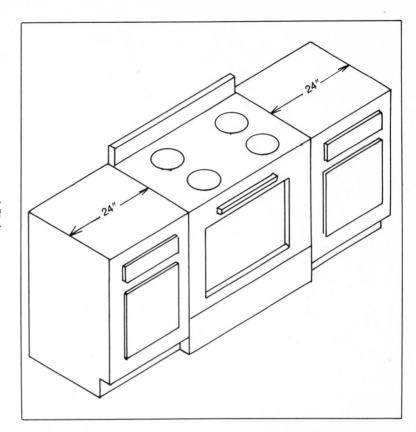

Fig. 2-2. The range or cooktop requires a minimum of 24 inches of counter on at least one side, preferably both.

preparation center can be combined with other areas, but larger rooms might have a separate area.

The preparation center is where most meals are actually prepared, encompassing many mixing, blending, cutting, and other food-preparation tasks. A counter of 36 to 42 inches is needed, along with storage for small appliances, mixing bowls, small utensils, and knives. If possible, the counter should have a surface that will not be marred by cutting and chopping operations; otherwise a separate cutting board should be available nearby.

Combining Work Centers

In kitchens where space is at a premium, it is sometimes necessary to combine work centers (Fig. 2-5) to create a compact, efficient kitchen in a limited area. Be sure, however, that the counter space is adequate.

As a general rule of thumb when combining work centers, the counter space provided for the combined area should be equal to the longest counter of the two, plus 1 foot. For example, suppose you wanted to combine the cooking center with the preparation center. The cooking center requires a minimum of 24 inches, and the preparation center requires 42 inches. Use the 42-inch requirement, and add 1 foot, or 12 inches. Therefore, the combined cooking/preparation center would require 54 inches of counter space.

If the countertop turns a corner, measure its total length along the front of the counter, not along the back to ensure that enough length is provided. The experts agree that no kitchen, no matter how compact or limited in space, should have less than 10 linear feet of base cabinets.

SPECIALIZED WORK CENTERS

Depending on the amount of available space and your preferences, you can incorporate one or more other work centers into the kitchen. These additional work

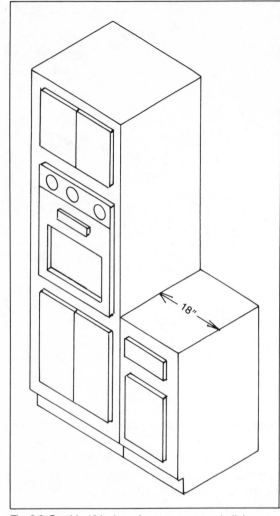

Fig. 2-3. Provide 18 inches of counter next to a built-in oven.

makes casual snacking a breeze, and it's the perfect setting for casual conversation with friends and family while cooking is being done. In smaller kitchens, the eating area often can serve double duty as a desk and meal-planning area, and might be a convenient spot for a telephone.

In many kitchens, the eating area is an extension of the countertops. This setup blends the area with the rest of the kitchen, offers additional counter space when needed for meal preparation, and conserves valuable floor space that would otherwise be lost to a table and chairs. An eating area such as this is commonly placed at one of three heights (Fig. 2-6):

☐ A counter raised above the level of the surrounding counters, usually at a height of 42 inches. A stool with a seat height of 30 to 32 inches would be used with this type of arrangement. The stool should have a footrest at about 12 inches off the floor, and 14 inches of knee space should be provided.
☐ A direct extension of the kitchen counters, at a height of 36 inches. For this height of counter, a 24-inch stool with a footrest at 6 inches is common, again with knee space of at least 14 inches.
☐ A counter lowered to 30 inches for use with a chair. In this arrangement, 20 inches of knee room should be provided.

For any of these eating counter arrangements, plan to provide an area 24 inches square for each person for comfortable dining, (Fig. 2-7), and allow 42 to 44 inches of room between the stools and any walls or other obstacles.

The Kitchen Office

In many of today's smaller homes, where unused space is at a premium, finding a convenient spot for a small home office might be a problem. For many people, the kitchen presents an ideal solution.

In the kitchen, an office can be incorporated into the existing cabinetry for a clean, blended look (Fig. 2-8). Lighting is good, and the work center is convenient to the main hub of the household. For meal planning, list making, letter, writing, and bill paying, you might find the kitchen a warm and cozy spot.

centers can make your kitchen more practical and usable, but remember that they consume space and, of course, their share of your kitchen budget dollar. Include specialized work centers only if their function is one for which you have an ongoing need.

Eating Areas

Perhaps the most common of the specialized kitchen work centers is the eating area. For cozy dining for two or complete family meals, the kitchen eating area is a convenient, workable arrangement for most kitchens, and one that's easily added. It

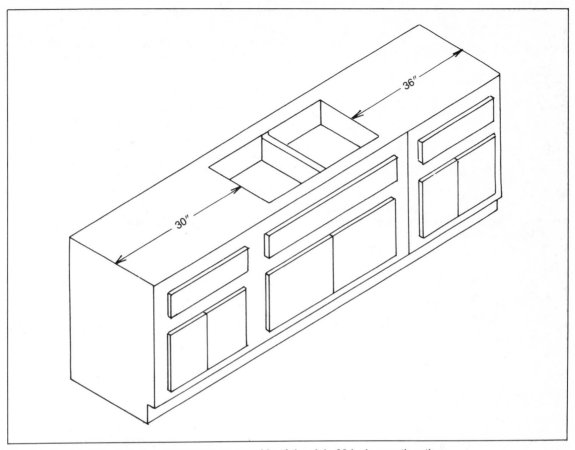

Fig. 2-4. Provide 30 inches of counterspace on one side of the sink, 36 inches on the other.

The kitchen office is usually no more than an open cabinet with a counter dropped to the standard desk height of 28 to 30 inches. The counter should be at, or near, the end of a run (Fig. 2-9), out of the main traffic and cooking areas, and should provide at least 30 to 36 inches of working space. You also might choose a wall opposite the main kitchen area, using cabinetry that matches or complements the rest of the kitchen. Many cabinet manufacturers offer desk units that match the rest of their cabinet lines.

The way you choose to set up and equip your kitchen office depends on your personal needs, but several things are common to most offices. You will need a smooth writing surface, such as wood or plastic laminate, and good lighting. Above the desk area is a good spot for a bulletin board to hold family mes-

sages and a shelf for cookbooks. Storage drawers should be handy for stationery and small office supplies, and there are swing-up tables that can handle your typewriter. The kitchen office is also a good spot for a telephone.

Another aspect of the kitchen office found in more homes is the computer. For everything from recipes to word processing, the home computer is a handy addition. Some cabinet manufacturers offer cabinetry specifically designed for housing the computer and printer. You also can try an office supply outlet or furniture store for a desk or table that complements the kitchen.

The Baking Center

If there's an avid baker in the house, a separate baking center might be just the thing to ensure

11

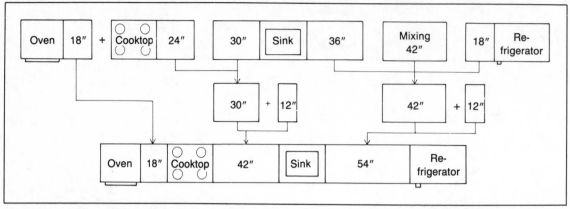

Fig. 2-5. Most kitchen designs require combining counterspaces. Take the larger space from each area and add 12 inches to it to ensure adequate counter area.

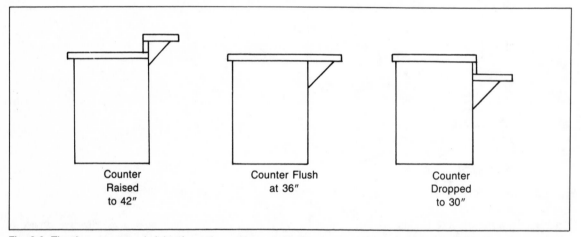

Fig. 2-6. The three common heights for eating counters, with the counter raised to 42 inches (left), the eating counter flush with the other counters at 36 inches (center), and the counter dropped to table height at 30 inches.

a continuous flow of home-baked goodies. As with the kitchen office, you can arrange the baking center to suit your needs, but certain things are essential.

You should plan to provide 36 to 42 inches or more of counter space. The counter can be at the standard height of 36 inches, or dropped to the 32-inch height that some bakers find more convenient (Fig. 2-10). If possible, construct all or at least part of the counters from wood or marble to provide an ideal surface for working with dough.

You will need cabinet space for bowls, baking sheets, and mixing utensils. Counter or cabinet space for a stand mixer, food processor, and other appliances is also handy. If you have limited counter space and a particularly heavy mixer, consider a swing-up stand that conveniently brings the mixer from storage in the cabinet up to working height at the counter.

Many bakers make provisions for bulk storage of such items as different flours and sugars. These supplies should be in closed containers or lined drawers, and might have dispensing spouts for convenient pouring. Closed plastic containers on wheels that can be rolled into the base cabinets are available through restaurant supply outlets.

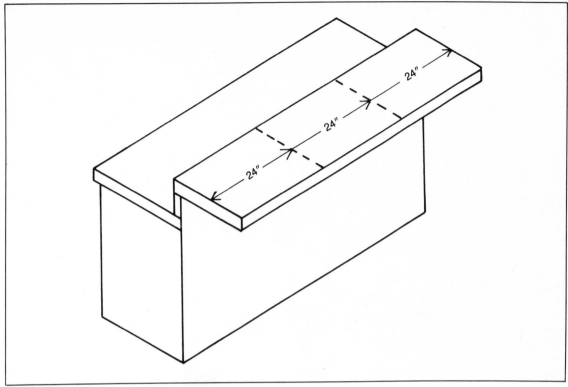

Fig. 2-7. Each space at the eating counter requires 24 inches of area.

THE WORK TRIANGLE

A very important concept in kitchen planning is the work triangle. The work triangle connects the three main kitchen work centers—refrigerator, cooking, and cleanup. A proper relationship between the three legs of the triangle is essential for efficiency (Fig. 2-11).

Kitchen-planning experts, through motion studies and other research, have determined the ideal dimensions of the triangle. If you keep these dimensions in mind at all times, you'll have an excellent guide to laying out a workable kitchen.

No leg of the triangle should be less than 4 feet in length, nor greater than 7 feet. Taken together, therefore, the three legs should not total less than 12 feet or more than 21 feet.

THE BASIC LAYOUTS

There are four basic layouts used in kitchen design (Fig. 2-11),with one optional variable that can be added to most arrangements. Your choice should be based on a number of factors, including the existing layout, the amount of space you have available, the existing and proposed traffic patterns, your available budget, and your preference.

Selecting a layout based on the room is usually the first step for most designers. In some cases, only one layout is possible, and will be clearly apparent. Quite often, however, more than one layout is possible. Exploring all the options will narrow it down to the best choice for you.

The One-Wall Kitchen

One-wall kitchens are the simplest and least expensive of all the design layouts. As the name implies, all the cabinets and appliances are laid out along one wall in a straight line. The work triangle is not possible with this arrangement, but the appliances are usually close enough together for efficiency. Remember the basic counter lengths noted previ-

13

ously, and avoid having any two work centers closer than 4 feet from each other.

The Corridor Kitchen

The corridor kitchen has the cabinet runs laid on two parallel walls, facing each other. This type of layout is efficient and permits a good work triangle. Because corner cabinets are eliminated and countertops are simplified, it is also one of the most economical kitchens to construct.

In laying out the corridor kitchen, keep in mind two important points:

☐ The two cabinet runs should be separated by at least 4 feet. If two people will be using the kitchen at the same time, increase the space to

Fig. 2-8. A kitchen office, beautifully blended in with the rest of the cabinets (Courtesy of Kitchen Kompact).

5 feet. Remember that spacing the runs too far apart is just as bad as having them too close together. Keep the maximum work triangle distances in mind, and use them as a guide.

☐ The kitchen should be arranged so that one end is closed off, or so that it dead-ends into a room that is not constantly in use, like a laundry room. Providing a doorway at both ends of the corridor kitchen, especially if one of them leads to the outside, creates a very busy and unworkable traffic pattern, which is the major complaint of people with this type of kitchen.

The L-Shaped Kitchen

Another very efficient layout is the L-shape, which has two adjacent runs of cabinets at right angles to each other. One leg of the L often forms a divider between rooms, and can easily be used as an eating counter. Traffic flow is usually good, as is the work triangle.

Take care in placing the major work centers. Avoid spacing them too far apart, which can be a very tiring layout. Most designers choose to place the sink between the refrigerator and the cooktop.

The U-Shaped Kitchen

It is almost universally agreed that the U-shape is the most efficient of all the kitchen layouts. Its shape eliminates the problem of through traffic; the counters are continuous around the room; and the three legs of the work triangle can easily be arranged into a very tight, workable layout.

Most designers choose to place the sink at the base of the U, with the refrigerator and the cooktop on the other two legs. As with the L-shape, either of the two side legs of the U can be extended out as a room divider and/or an eating area.

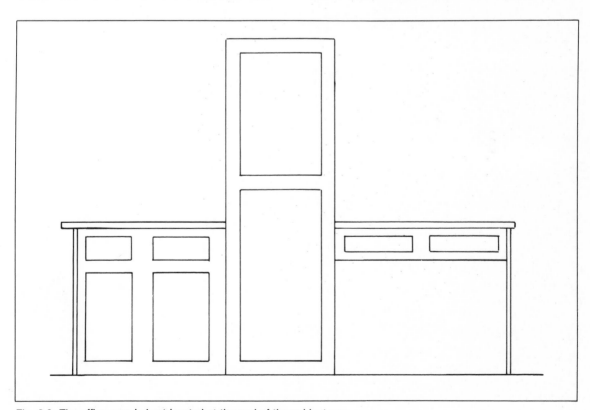

Fig. 2-9. The office area is best located at the end of the cabinet run.

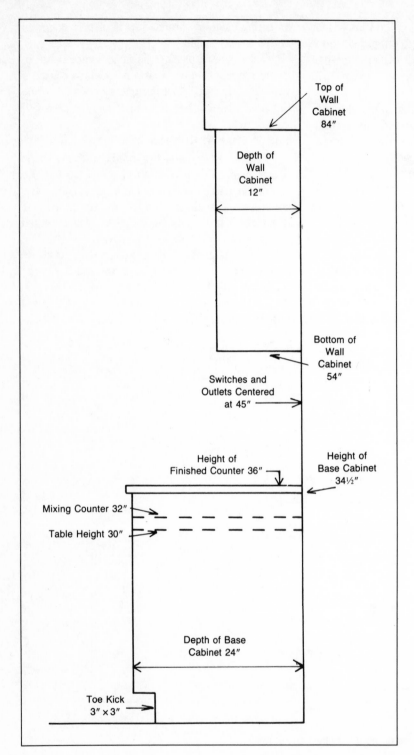

Top of
Wall
Cabinet
84″

Depth of
Wall
Cabinet
12″

Bottom of
Wall
Cabinet
54″

Switches and
Outlets Centered
at 45″

Height of
Finished Counter 36″

Height of
Base Cabinet
34½″

Mixing Counter 32″

Table Height 30″

Depth of Base
Cabinet 24″

Toe Kick
3″ × 3″

Fig. 2-10. Standard kitchen cabinet sizes and heights.

16

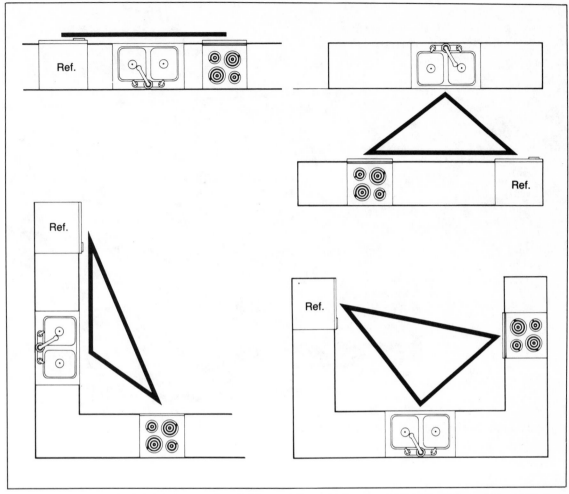

Fig. 2-11. The four standard kitchen layouts: One wall (upper left), corridor (upper right), L-shape (lower left), and U-shape (Courtesy of Scheirich Cabinetry).

There are a few disadvantages to the U-shape. It requires the most room: at least 6 feet are needed between the legs of the U. It also takes a large number of cabinets, including corner cabinets, and a large amount of countertop material. It is, therefore, usually the most expensive of the layouts to construct.

The Island Kitchen

An *island* is a freestanding cabinet or set of cabinets, used with one of the basic layouts to provide additional working and storage space. Uses for the island are unlimited; it might contain one of the work centers, it might be used as an eating area, or it might be just additional cabinet and counter space.

The island is usually placed in the center of the room and is permanently fixed in place, although some smaller types are on wheels (Fig. 2-12). An island can be used with any of the basic layouts, including being placed on the end wall of the corridor, but it is most commonly associated with the L- and U-shaped kitchens. If the island is to contain the sink or cooktop, it then becomes one point on the work triangle and needs to be planned accordingly.

Fig. 2-12. A portable island cabinet, which rolls on casters to wherever it's needed (Courtesy of Kitchen Kompact).

Chapter 3

Space Considerations

IT'S NOW NECESSARY FOR YOU, OR YOUR DESIGNER, to apply the kitchen planning principles to your kitchen. Many different things come into play at this point—your ideas and tastes, the specific needs of you and your family, the layout you want, your budget, and the available space—all with an eye toward a kitchen that really works for you!

The better you've done your homework from Chapters 1 and 2, the better you'll know yourself and your needs. You probably already have a particular look in mind, and perhaps a layout has presented itself. So now, what about space? Just how much room do you have to work with, and how much do you need?

Most of your planning at this point revolves around two things: your needs, as defined in Chapter 1, and the space you have available.

SPACE NEEDS

It's difficult to say just how much space is enough for a kitchen, although most experts agree that 100 to 160 square feet is about right for most layouts. Your own needs for counter and storage space are a factor, as are the appliances you wish to install, the work centers you want, the layout you've chosen, and, of course, your budget. Bigger isn't always better, but it is always more expensive.

Cabinets, counters, flooring—it all adds up, and the bigger the room, the more of everything you'll need.

This is where your questionnaires and lists really come into play. By clearly defining your needs and desires, you'll know how to get what you really want out of your new kitchen, without skimping on necessary features and without going overboard on unneeded extras. One of the tricks at this point is not to get caught up in the excitement of remodeling. It is exciting, especially if a new kitchen has been a dream for a long time. Be practical, but on the other hand, be sure you get what you want!

EXISTING VS. ADDED SPACE

Probably the biggest question facing you and your designer at this point is whether your space needs can be met within the existing room, or whether more space should be added. Several options usually present themselves, depending on the size and floor plan of the house. As with the selection of a basic layout, the one that's right for you will quickly become apparent.

Existing Space

A new cabinet arrangement with a more efficient appliance layout might be just what you need, per-

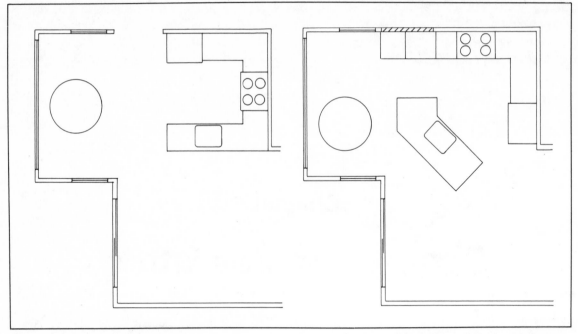

Fig. 3-1. This kitchen, which shared space with an adjoining family room, was easily expanded within the existing area without having to add or steal space. The only structural change was the closing off of a little-used doorway (right) (Design courtesy of Kitchen Concepts).

haps with the addition of an island. Chances are it can be accomplished within the existing room (Fig. 3-1). This is, in most instances, the least expensive approach. It requires the least amount of carpentry, plumbing, electrical wiring, and other work.

Gaining Space From Adjacent Rooms

A method that's popular with a lot of designers when dealing with the too-small kitchen is stealing space from adjacent rooms. There are many ways of doing this, and it can be a simple and very effective way of gaining space. In many cases it's inexpensive to accomplish, and acts to apportion the home's existing space in the most useful and practical manner.

Stealing space might be as simple as opening up a small pantry into an adjacent garage (Fig. 3-2), swallowing up an unused closet, or perhaps it might involve expanding out into one or even several rooms. The key factors are the home's layout, how much space you need to gain, and how much you can afford to give up out of the adjacent rooms.

The first step is to carefully survey the rooms and spaces directly adjacent to the kitchen, including closets, pantrys, even outside storage spaces. Make a sketch showing the kitchen and these surrounding areas, and try to visualize how and where the kitchen might be expanded.

A perfect area for stealing space is from the dining room or dining area (Fig. 3-3). Formal dining rooms were a regular feature in older homes, however these areas are rarely used today. Their space can be much better utilized. A common design approach for many designers is to combine the kitchen with the dining area, and then incorporate an attached kitchen eating center as discussed in Chapter 2. The result of this approach is a greatly expanded kitchen, a roomy, open feeling to the room, and a practical eating area that gets more use than the original dining area.

If your kitchen is adjacent to an attached garage, this is often another perfect expansion area. In most instances, a few feet can be stolen from the garage area without interfering with the cars. This area

20

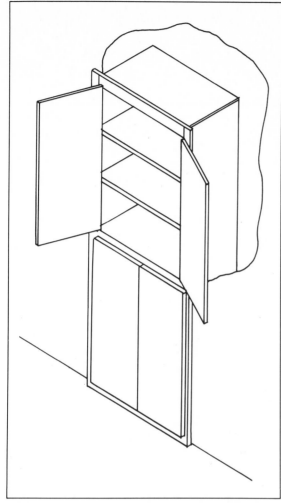

Fig. 3-2. A two-foot-deep pantry cabinet can easily be recessed into an adjacent garage or closet, with only the faceframe and doors exposed into the kitchen.

might be just what you need to create a walk-in pantry (Fig. 3-4), appliance garage, or laundry area, or even to increase the width or depth of the entire kitchen.

Adding Space

The other alternative when more space is needed is to add it onto the existing house. Room additions can be expensive and time consuming, since they require a foundation, exterior wall covering, roofing, and all the other elements of the origi-

nal structure. They also require careful planning to make the addition blend in with the house and avoid a tacked on look.

Room additions have the advantage of allowing you to add exactly as much space as you need without sacrificing it from other areas. In many cases, additional rooms are added at the same time—a much needed new bathroom, for example, or an expanded master suite—which adds space, comfort, and value to the entire home (Figs. 3-5 and 3-6).

If a room addition appears to be the answer in your situation, there are several items to take into consideration. Of primary importance is whether the kitchen is on an outside wall, adjacent to a portion of the yard where expansion is possible. If not, entire rooms may need to be rearranged and the kitchen placed elsewhere, which can get prohibitively expensive.

Other things to consider are the property line setbacks, which are usually 25 feet in the front and back and 5 to 10 feet on the sides. Check with the building department or planning commission to get the exact setbacks for your area, then measure carefully to determine if you have the necessary room to expand. You'll also need to consider how the roof lines will align, if the siding can be matched, and other aesthetic considerations. The services of a professional designer might be a worthwhile expense if considering an addition.

As your ideas begin to come together, you should write them down. Some basic sketches are quite helpful during the planning stages, and finished drawings will be necessary for the actual construction.

Sketching to Scale

While any type of sketching is useful when you're thinking about your kitchen and discussing the options, scale sketches will be necessary early on to see exactly how the kitchen is coming together. The easiest way to draw a scale sketch is with graph paper (Fig. 3-7).

Graph paper is available at most stationery, office, and art supply stores, and is simply paper which has been accurately ruled into a grid pattern, creating a number of uniform squares. Different sizes of

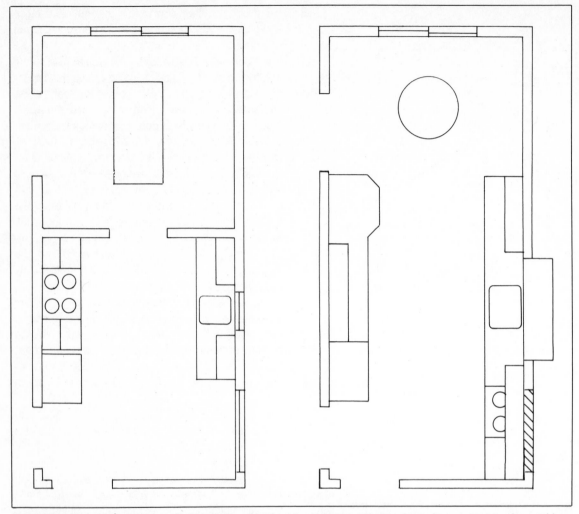

Fig. 3-3. An example of stealing space. The kitchen at left had few cabinets and a shortage of counterspace, plus a seldom-used formal dining room with a large rectangular table. The remodeled kitchen combines both rooms by removing the wall, then closes in one window, adds a large garden window over the sink, and utilizes an eating counter and a smaller, round table.

squares are available, but four or eight to the inch are the most useful for this type of sketching.

Using paper with four squares per inch, you can let each square (¼ inch) equal 6 inches. This is ½-inch scale because ½ inch (2 squares) equals 1 foot in this scale. With paper having eight squares per inch, each square will equal 3 inches.

You now have a useful scale for your drawings. As your planning becomes more precise and you begin to take exact measurements of the kitchen, you can use the graph paper to lay out accurate line lengths.

Final Drawings

A well-prepared set of plans is necessary for taking out building permits, obtaining contractor bids, and guiding construction. Kitchen remodeling does not require as complex and detailed plans as those prepared for constructing a house, since no structural details are usually necessary. The kitchen

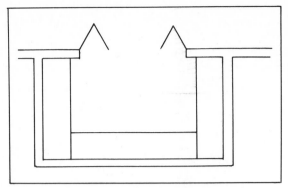

Fig. 3-4. A walk-in pantry with bifold doors, which can be built in to an adjacent garage or other room.

plans should, however, be neatly drawn in ½-inch or ¼-inch scale, and should contain enough information for building officials and contractors to understand the details of the project.

You will need a floor plan that shows how the new kitchen will look, including any structural details such as doorways to be filled in or walls to be added or opened up. Included on the floor plan, or on a separate drawing, should be complete electrical details as discussed in Chapters 6 and 9. The floor plan should also show a detailed layout of the cabinets, including filler pieces, to guide their installation. Cabinet layouts are described in detail in Chapter 5.

To further help with the installation and to make it easier to visualize what the finished kitchen will look like, elevations are helpful (Fig. 3-8). These elevations can take the form of a perspective drawing that shows the kitchen in three-dimensional form, or a straight on look at each wall individually. If you are having a designer do the kitchen, they will prepare all of the necessary drawings for you.

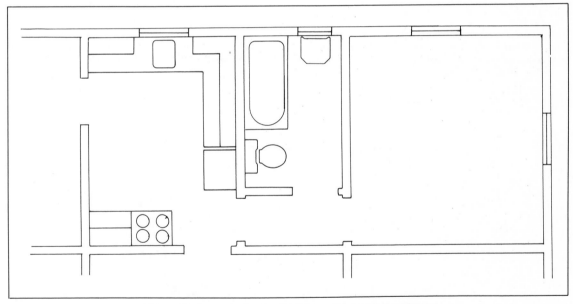

Fig. 3-5. Before the room addition, this house had a small kitchen and only one bathroom.

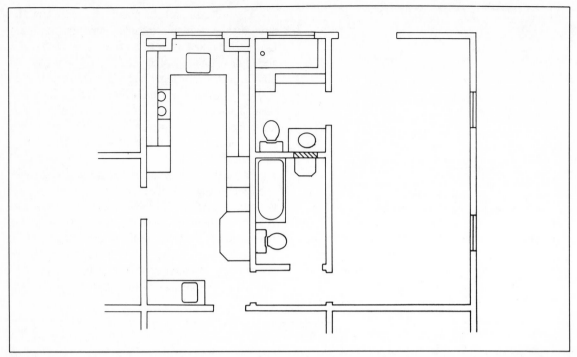

Fig. 3-6. After the addition, the kitchen is greatly expanded, as is the master bedroom at right. A new master bathroom with sunken tub has also been added. In this case, the addition solved several of the home's problems at once.

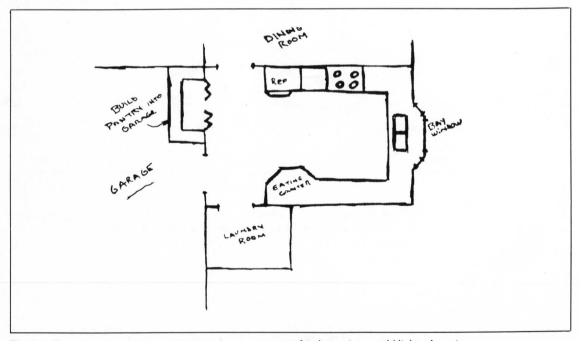

Fig. 3-7. Sketching to scale on graph paper is an easy way of trying out several kitchen layouts.

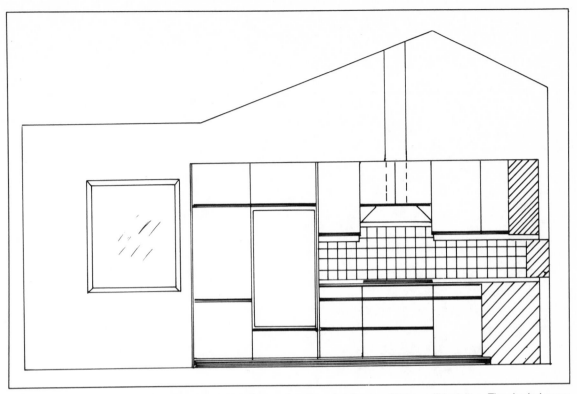

Fig. 3-8. Elevation drawings such as this one can help you visualize what the new kitchen will look like. The shaded areas at the right indicate where the adjacent cabinet run will intersect (Design courtesy of Kitchen Concepts).

Chapter 4

Appliance Selection and Placement

A NEW KITCHEN USUALLY MEANS NEW APPLIances. It's the ideal time to replace worn-out models, and to update with new features. It also might be the time to add new appliances, like a microwave oven, that were lacking in the old kitchen. New appliances represent a major expense. The model you choose is one you'll be living with for some time to come, so you need to choose wisely.

If you are adding new appliances or changing the size or type of fuel used in existing appliances, other work may be involved that needs to be considered. New or larger capacity electrical circuits might be necessary, for example, or a new gas line. Locations might need to be moved, or new venting provided for. All these things should be taken into consideration and planned for from the beginning, to avoid unnecessary problems and expenses later. If you have doubts about what you'll need for a particular appliance, check with your appliance dealer.

REFRIGERATOR/FREEZERS

The main criteria in selecting a refrigerator/freezer is size. The ratings are in cubic feet, which is the inside storage area's width × height × depth. You should plan to select a refrigerator that provides sufficient storage for at least a week's supply of food.

The standard choice in refrigerator/freezers is between the one-door and the two-door models, a choice which is essentially governed by size. Smaller one-door refrigerators have a small freezer located behind an inside door. They are often limited to no more than about 14 cubic feet, and often are manually defrosted. Besides the space limitations and manual defrost, it is necessary to open the refrigerator door every time you need something out of the freezer.

More popular are the two-door models, which are available in sizes up to approximately 27 cubic feet. The choices here are the side-by-side, which has the freezer next to the refrigerator, and the top freezer model, which has the freezer above the refrigerator. The majority of two-door models are self-defrosting. This increases the unit's initial cost and its energy consumption; however, it is a worthwhile feature for most people.

There are a number of optional features available with today's refrigerator/freezers. Some models have a separate door within the main refrigerator door, allowing access to frequently used items without opening the main door. Vegetable crispers, meat and cheese storage, various adjustable door shelf combinations, and different interior storage compartments are all common features.

Perhaps the most common option is the automatic icemaker. Fresh water is supplied to a unit within the freezer compartment, which cycles on and off to provide a constant supply of ice. Some models dispense the ice through the door, others supply chilled water and even crushed ice. The main thing to remember is that refrigerators of this type require a separate water line, which should be provided during the construction process.

Some of the larger, more expensive refrigerators also come with optional door panel inserts. This allows you to insert stained wood panels, colored panels, cloth, wallpaper, laminates, and other decorative materials to match or compliment the decor of the kitchen.

Freezers

The freezer area in the combination refrigerator/freezer is relatively small, and is not intended for long term food storage. For long-term, bulk food storage, a separate freezer is the best solution. This separate freezer may be placed in the kitchen with the refrigerator, but is usually located in a utility room, pantry, or even in the garage.

There are two basic styles in freezers: upright, which has a vertical door and resembles a refrigerator, and chest, which is approximately waist high and has a horizontal door on top. Upright models offer easier viewing of the contents and greater storage convenience. The chest models offer storage for larger items. The other selection criteria is size, which ranges from as little as 5 cubic feet to 27 cubic feet or more. Most styles are manually defrosted.

As a general rule of thumb, you can plan on needing a minimum of 4½ cubic feet of storage space for each family member. A family of four, therefore, would require a freezer at least 18 cubic feet in size.

If you purchase or put up foods in bulk, allow extra room.

Refrigerator Placement

Most refrigerator/freezers are available as right hand door or left hand door models, and some are reversible. The refrigerator should be placed so that the adjacent counter space is on the handle side of the door, allowing convenient loading and unloading.

A minimum of 36 inches should be provided from the front of the refrigerator to any obstacles (Fig. 4-1). This space allows sufficient room for you to stand in front of the unit and have easy access to the interior. Remember during the planning stages that a refrigerator is usually 26 to 30 inches deep, not the standard 24 inches of most base cabinets.

COOKING EQUIPMENT

There are a number of options available to you when selecting cooking equipment. You can choose a range, which is a combination cooktop and oven in one unit, or a cooktop and oven as separate units.

Ranges may be *freestanding*, which means they have their own feet and sit on the floor between two cabinets, or they may be drop-in, where they rest on the surrounding countertops. Freestanding ranges also offer the options of the oven below the cooktop, the oven above the cooktop, or both. Finally, you can choose between electric and natural gas models.

The drop-in cooktop also offers the choice between gas and electricity. Four-burner models are the most common, but six-burner models are also available. Some of the more expensive units have interchangeable cartridges that let you switch between burners, griddles, a barbecue grill, and other options. Look for a unit with at least two large burners. The less expensive models with one large and three small burners can be very inconvenient for most cooks.

A relative newcomer is the magnetic induction cooktop. It utilizes electromagnets to heat metal cookware, so the heat is only in the pot and the contents. The cooktop is totally smooth and, except for

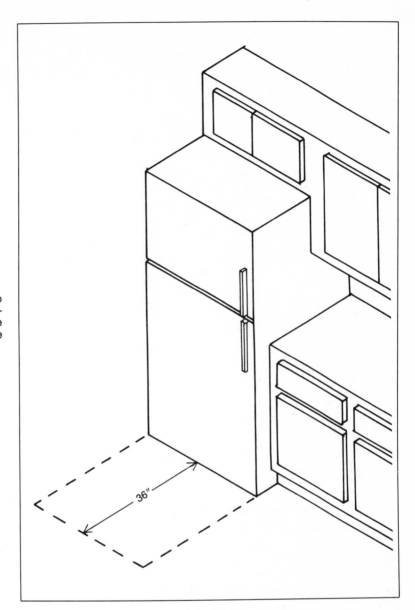

Fig. 4-1. At least 36 inches needs to be provided in front of the refrigerator. Measure from the face of the refrigerator, not from the face of the cabinets.

36"

reflected heat from the pot, stays completely cool. The units are still expensive at this time, and utensils must be iron or magnetic steel.

Separate oven choices include single ovens, double ovens, conventional oven/microwave oven combinations, conventional oven/convection oven combinations, and others. You need to know what you want and need out of an oven, and choose ac-

cordingly. As with other aspects of kitchen planning, you want to be sure and get what you need, but not waste money on features you won't use.

For most cooks, a single oven is sufficient. If you have a large family or do a lot of entertaining, a double oven might be worth considering. The avid baker might want to look into a convection oven, which uses an internal fan to circulate warm air for

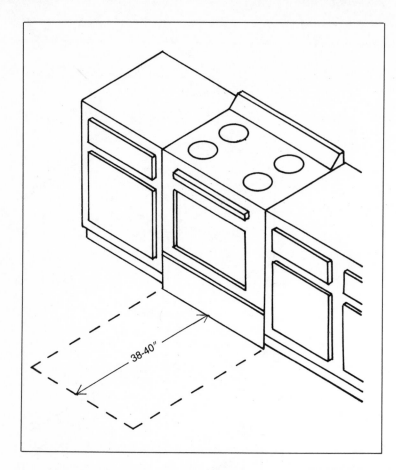

Fig. 4-2. Provide 38 to 40 inches in front of the range for easy access to the oven compartment.

even baking. Built-in temperature probes, slow cook elements, automatic timers, and built-in rotisseries are some other common optional features.

Another popular option is the self-cleaning oven. There are two types—continuous cleaning, which cleans while the oven is in regular use, and pyrolitic, which has a separate, high heat cleaning cycle that is more effective on large spills. Either one is a nice feature to consider.

Barbecues

Built-in barbecues and grills are a popular feature for the cook who likes grilled food. Electric and gas units are available, as are live coal models. If considering a live coal unit, remember that adequate ventilation must be provided, as the fumes can be toxic.

Cooking Equipment Placement

Freestanding ranges vary in width from 20 or 21 inches to 42 inches, with depths of 25 inches for most units and 26 to 28 inches for high/low models. Cooktops are 12 to 24 inches wide for two-burner models, 30 to 42 inches wide for four-burner units, and 36 to 48 inches wide for models with six burners. Separate oven units are 24 to 28 inches wide.

For access to a freestanding or drop-in range, plan on providing at least 38 to 40 inches from the front of the unit to the nearest obstacle (Fig. 4-2). Separate oven units, which sit in a higher cabinet, require 36 inches of clearance (Fig. 4-3). Whenever possible, 48 inches of clearance from the front of the range or oven to the nearest obstacle is preferable.

If you have a barbecue grill and the primary cook in the kitchen will be using both the grill and the

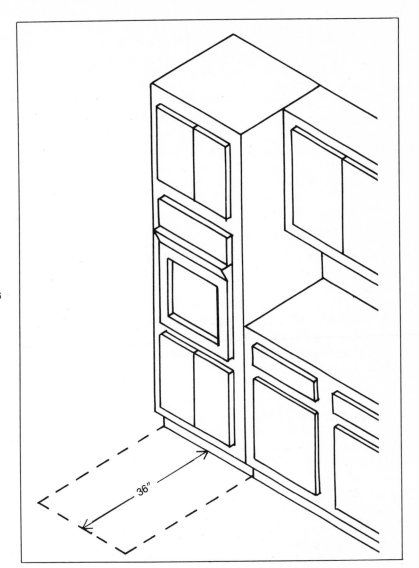

Fig. 4-3. A built-in oven requires 36 inches of clearance in front of it.

36"

cooktop, the best location is to have them side by side. (Do not place a gas grill next to a downward ventilating cooktop, as the flame can be drawn into the fan.) If the second cook in a two-cook kitchen is using the grill, place it away from the main traffic areas, and provide separate storage and utensils.

MICROWAVE OVENS

Once considered an expensive extra, microwave ovens are becoming an almost universally accepted fea-

ture in today's kitchens. For warming and defrosting, heating snacks and quick meals for the kids, or cooking complete meals, these versatile ovens are well worth adding to your kitchen remodeling plans.

Microwave ovens cook by generating waves of electromagnetic energy that cycle back and forth millions of times per second. The waves pass through items like glass and plastic and are absorbed by the food. The waves cause water molecules within the food to rotate back and forth with the cycles. This rotation creates friction, which in turn creates heat that cooks the food from the inside out.

Microwave ovens range in size from about ½ to 1½ cubic feet, with power on the high setting ranging from 450 to 750 watts. The most basic models have two power levels and a simple minute/second timer. The more expensive units have variable power settings, digital timers, temperature probes, and browning units. The choice of the right model for you depends on the type of cooking you do.

Microwave Oven Placement

Being essentially a portable unit, finding the right place in the kitchen for a microwave oven can present a problem. Left on the counter, they can use up a lot of counter space, and are difficult to clean under. They are, however, too large to fit in a standard upper cabinet at eye level.

One solution has been to combine the microwave with a conventional oven in the same oven cabinet. Oven cabinets have sufficient depth and height to contain the microwave unit, and as long as the microwave and the conventional oven are laid out in the cabinet at the same time to ensure proper spacing, the installation should present no problem. An oven cabinet could be used to house the microwave alone, without the conventional oven below it.

The height of the unit in the cabinet is a matter of personal preference. Kitchen experts have stated that for safe use, the shelf of the microwave should be no higher than the height of the user's shoulder. A more convenient height, if used in a cabinet without the conventional oven, would be at the approximate height of the user's elbow.

Another solution to installing the microwave is the special microwave oven cabinet offered by most cabinet manufacturers. This is essentially a wall cabinet, but it has the greater depth needed to accommodate the microwave. The cabinet should be placed so that the microwave oven is at a convenient height. This placement will vary with the height of the individual cabinet.

Microwave ovens need to breathe in normal operation; that is, they take in and exhaust air through louvers in the outside case. For installation in a cabinet, an air space needs to be provided around the case. Most manufacturers offer an installation kit for use when building one of their portable units into a permanent installation.

The installation kit usually consists of a chrome or stainless steel frame with vents, and often some type of feet or spacers to raise the oven. Follow the manufacturer's recommendations carefully when building in any microwave, and be sure to use the installation kit approved for their unit.

If the microwave is used primarily by the main cook in the kitchen, it should be placed within the work triangle for most efficient use. Even though a separate conventional oven may be placed outside the triangle, the work habits associated with the microwave contradict the rule. If, however, the microwave is used mainly by snackers or by the second cook in a two-cook kitchen, it is best placed outside the regular traffic patterns of the kitchen.

Approximately 24 inches of counter space needs to be provided. This could be the same space used by the conventional oven, or could be created by placing a pull-out cutting board in the cabinet below the microwave (unless the microwave has a bottom-hinged door).

DISHWASHERS

The automatic dishwasher has long been an accepted feature of the well-equipped kitchen. The designs have stayed relatively the same for quite some time, with the advent of microelectronic controls and better soundproofing being the only major changes in recent years.

Any basic dishwasher model will do just that—wash dishes. As you move up the line, you'll get additional controls; quieter operation; soft food disposers to reduce the amount of rinsing necessary; cycles to handle pots, pans, and burnt-on food; adjustable racks; and other interior features. You can spend a little or a lot, depending on what features you need.

Most dishwashers come with reversible color panels for the doors, allowing you to quickly change panels to match the other appliances in the kitchen. You can also insert optional wooden door panels,

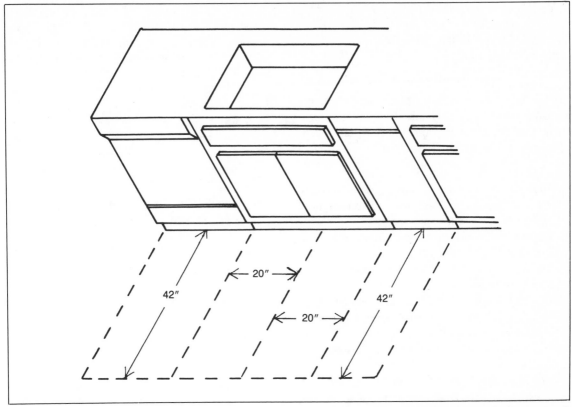

Fig. 4-4. Provide 42 inches of clearance in front of a dishwasher or trash compactor, plus at least 20 inches next to it for loading access.

wallpaper, or other decorative materials to achieve the look you desire.

If you currently have a portable dishwasher that you would like to build into the cabinets, most manufacturers offer a simple conversion kit. The installation of this kit is a matter of removing the top, installing a valve in place of the hoses, and replacing the casters with adjustable feet. The unit should then be able to be placed in a 24-inch opening like the standard built-in model.

Dishwasher Placement

The dishwasher should be placed directly next to the sink, if possible. It should be situated with at least 20 inches next to the open door for easy loading, and with a clearance of at least 42 inches from the front of the unit to the nearest obstacle (Fig. 4-4).

Try to avoid placing the dishwasher directly in a corner, or around the corner from the sink. If this is unavoidable, be sure to place a filler strip next to the dishwasher to create clearance for the door to open without striking the adjacent cabinets.

TRASH COMPACTORS

A relative newcomer to the kitchen, the trash compactor can be a handy addition. It compresses dry garbage to about ¼ its normal volume, greatly reducing the number of trips out to the garbage can. Like dishwashers, the features are relatively the same from model to model. Look for one with convenient loading, easy bag removal, and a deodorizer. Portable units can be converted to built-in use with a manufacturer's kit, and fit in the area of a 15-inch-wide cabinet.

The standard location for the trash compactor

is on the opposite side of the sink from the dishwasher. As with the dishwasher, 20 inches should be provided next to the unit for easy loading, and the same care should be taken with corner locations.

OTHER APPLIANCES

The kitchen is a haven for built-in appliances, ranging from just the basics in some kitchens to everything invented by man in others. Here are a few other appliances worth considering:

☐ Garbage Disposal: Virtually standard in today's kitchen, the garbage disposal grinds up and washes away most food wastes. The main features here are motor size and quiet operation. Garbage disposals are made to fit any standard 3½ inch sink drain opening, so placement in a two or three compartment sink is a matter of personal preference.

   Two words of caution when purchasing a garbage disposal. If you have never had one in this kitchen before, it's best to have the waste lines from the sink snaked out before installation. Grease built up in the lines can close off the inside diameter of the pipes, causing them to clog quickly when the greater volume of waste associated with a garbage disposal is introduced into them. Also, use the garbage disposal sparingly if you are on a septic system. Too much fibrous solid waste can clog the leach lines and create serious problems with the system.

☐ Built-in Toaster/Built-in Can Opener: Two popular and relatively inexpensive items are the built-in toaster and the built-in can opener. Both units have a metal can which is fastened to the wall studs and wired during construction. The toaster or can opener mechanism then slips into the can

and is locked in place. These units can be placed just about anywhere, and a careful study of your work habits should indicate the best spot. Do not place the toaster under an undercabinet light, as the heat from the toaster can damage the light's plastic diffuser.

☐ Hot Water Dispensers: If you use a lot of very hot water for soup, tea, or general cooking, this is a real time saver. It has a separate dispensing head and an under-sink heating tank for instant hot water in the 190° F. range whenever you need it. Plan to provide an additional electrical outlet under the sink (don't use the one from the garbage disposal, since it's controlled by a switch), and an additional outlet on the hot water stop valve to connect to the dispenser's water line.

COMMERCIAL EQUIPMENT

There is often a temptation to purchase heavy duty commercial restaurant equipment for home use. Experienced kitchen designers warn that there are some serious disadvantages to consider.

Commercial equipment is large and heavy, often over 29 inches deep and weighing in the neighborhood of 500 to 800 pounds. As a result, placement in the room is very difficult. A larger gas supply is required. The heat generated from these units requires heat-proof coverings on the walls and floor, and strains the home's air conditioning system. Extra ventilation is required for these bigger grills, and many of the components will not fit in a standard sink for washing.

If you are considering commercial equipment, be sure you discuss the specific requirements with your dealer and plan for them accordingly.

Chapter 5

Laying Out the Cabinets

NOW THAT YOU KNOW YOUR NEEDS AND YOUR available work space, you can proceed with laying out the cabinets on paper. This step requires careful measuring and may involve making several attempts at the layout until you have it right. The effort you put in here will save you countless hours and problems on the job.

If you are removing a wall or constructing an addition, it is best to have this work completed first for the most accurate measurements. It's not always possible to work directly from an architect's or designer's plans, since the actual measurements of the finished room may vary from the plans by several inches.

In the case where you are removing a wall to expand the kitchen into an adjoining room, it's usually possible to take accurate measurements and leave the wall intact. If the wall is standard construction, it will be 2-×-4 framing with ½-inch drywall on each side. The actual width of a 2 × 4 is 3½ inches, so the total wall thickness is 4½ inches. You can measure up to the wall being removed, add 4½ inches, then begin measuring again from the other side (Fig. 5-1).

If you are unsure as to the wall's construction, select an area away from any electrical wiring and bore a small hole through the wall (Fig. 5-2). Insert a dowel or other object through the hole so that it protrudes through each side of the wall, and make a pencil mark on the dowel against the wall on both sides. The distance between the marks is the thickness of the wall.

CUSTOM CABINETS

You have two basic choices for your cabinets, custom and modular. Each choice offers certain advantages and disadvantages. Custom cabinets are those constructed specifically for your kitchen by a cabinet shop. They will send someone out to measure your kitchen exactly, and will discuss what you want and need in your finished cabinets. The shop will usually have a number of door samples for you to choose from, along with wood types, stain colors, and finishes.

The obvious advantage is that the cabinets are a custom fit for your kitchen, with all the features you want built in. The shop does the installing and finishing, with little for the do-it-yourselfer to worry about. The disadvantages are usually the cost, which can range from slightly to considerably higher than modular cabinets, and, unless the shop is a large one, your choices in styles may be limited.

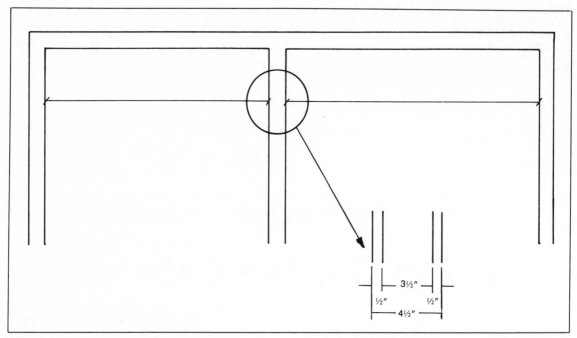

Fig. 5-1. When you are removing a wall between two rooms, take cabinet measurements by measuring each room and then adding in the thickness of the wall.

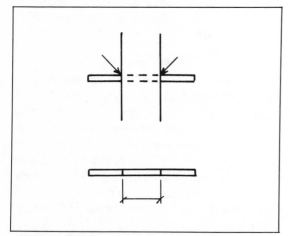

Fig. 5-2. If you don't know the wall's thickness, insert a dowel through a hole drilled in the wall, mark both sides, then measure between the marks.

If you choose to go with a custom cabinet shop, be sure you see a sample of their work in advance, preferably a completely installed kitchen. One or two door samples is not enough to judge the quality of workmanship that needs to be maintained over the entire job, including the installation. Get a firm estimate, with all of the specifications spelled out in detail. You'll be asked to put down a deposit, which is normal, but don't pay for the entire job in advance.

MODULAR CABINETS

Modular cabinets get their name from the fact that they are manufactured as individual units, not as a complete run like custom cabinets are. Different widths and heights are connected together on the job site to make up a run of the necessary length, with the odd inches and fractions being made up by fillers or special corner cabinets.

There are a number of quality manufacturers of modular cabinets, offering a tremendous variety of styles in every price range. Some of the cabinets built primarily of particleboard, found at the low end of some manufacturer's lines, are not really worth dealing with, as the quality and durability are low. But most of the cabinets in the mid and upper price ranges, constructed of plywood and top grade hardwoods, rival the quality of anything put out by the custom shops.

The advantages and disadvantages of the modular cabinets tend to be the opposite of those of custom cabinets. You will normally pay less for the same amount of modular cabinets, since they are manufactured in volume to keep individual prices down. The installation is within the range of most skilled do-it-yourselfers, so there's a potential savings in installation, also. Choice is another advantage. Most manufacturers offer 10 or 15 different lines, each with a distinctive look and finish.

The main drawback is in losing some of the custom look, and perhaps some of the custom features. The modular cabinets are factory prefinished, so custom blended paint or stain colors are usually impossible. And while most manufacturers offer a full line of roll-out shelves, wine racks, and other features, you may not be able to get all the custom extras you'd like. In some cases however, just to confuse the issue, you may find more built-in features with modular cabinets than you can get with custom cabinets (Fig. 5-3).

All in all, today's modular cabinets compare quite favorably with custom work. Study the various lines carefully, look at a number of samples (or a complete kitchen if you can), and weigh all the pros and cons before making the choice for your kitchen.

MEASURING YOUR KITCHEN

Getting the kitchen measured correctly and accurately is a critical step. It ensures that your subsequent planning is right, and that the cabinets you order will look and fit the way you expect. You will need a good quality tape measure at least 12 feet long, a pencil, and graph paper with four or eight squares to the inch. You will be working with a scale of ½ inch equals 1 foot.

Begin your measuring by taking the overall dimensions of the room. Remember to measure from wall to wall, not between the baseboards, which can throw you off by several inches. To ensure accuracy, measure from one corner to an even numbered spot on the wall, say 10 feet, and mark this spot (Fig. 5-4). Measure from the other corner to this mark, and add 10 feet to the measurement.

Draw out the overall perimeter of the room on your graph paper. Outside the lines of the walls,

write down the measurements (Fig. 5-5), working to the nearest fraction of an inch. Now you are ready to begin taking detailed measurements. Kitchen Kompact, Inc., a manufacturer of modular cabinets, offers these recommendations for measuring the rest of the room:

☐ Place the rule against the wall at a height of about 36 inches and measure from one corner to the nearest door or window. Measure to the edge of the trim. (You might also wish to note the measurement from the corner to the centerline of the window, which is often helpful when laying out the cabinets.)

☐ Note this measurement to the nearest fraction of an inch on your paper. Also measure the width of the trim and check on the possibility of cutting it down if necessary.

☐ Note the swing of each door and label doors according to where they lead. Measure the width of each door and window and note this on the measurement layout.

☐ Measure from the floor to the bottom of the window sill. This is essential to determine the height of the backsplash (for certain types of countertops). Note the possibility of cutting down the sill if necessary.

☐ Measure the height of the room from floor to ceiling, noting it on your sketch. It's a good idea to check this measurement in two diagonally opposite corners to see if you will have to allow for a floor that is out of level.

☐ Check the square of the room. Get someone to help you measure wall to wall about 36 inches up from the floor. This will tell you if the walls are bowed or out of square. Always check the corners with a square.

☐ Note the size and location of radiators, registers, or other appliances and fixtures. Note electrical and plumbing locations.

☐ Note the width, height, and depth of all appliances (new or existing that you're reusing), including handles and hardware, and show the swing of doors of these appliances. Indicate how appliances such as refrigerators are hinged. Doors with outside hinges, as on some types of refriger-

Fig. 5-3. Some of the accessories available from one manufacturer of modular cabinets (Courtesy of Scheirich Cabinetry).

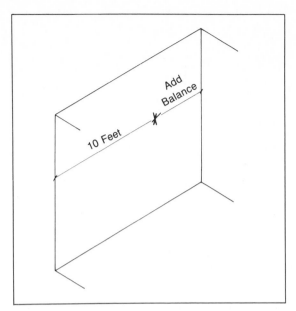

Fig. 5-4. To accurately measure a room, first measure out from one wall, then from the other and add the two measurements.

ators, swing back further and will require more clearance.

COMMON MODULAR CABINETS

Before you attempt the cabinet layout, take a moment to familiarize yourself with the different general types of cabinets that are offered, and also any specific variations your chosen manufacturer has available:

Wall Cabinets

Wall cabinets are the upper cabinets which are mounted on the wall or from the ceiling, above the countertops (Fig. 5-6). The basic wall cabinet is 12 inches deep, 30 inches high, and comes in widths of 9 inches up to 48 inches, in 3-inch increments. Shorter wall cabinets are used where extra clearance is needed over a range, cooktop, or refrigerator, or anywhere added clearance over the counter is required. Common heights are 12, 15 (standard

Fig. 5-5. Make a sketch on graph paper and note all of the pertinent measurements (Courtesy of Scheirich Cabinetry).

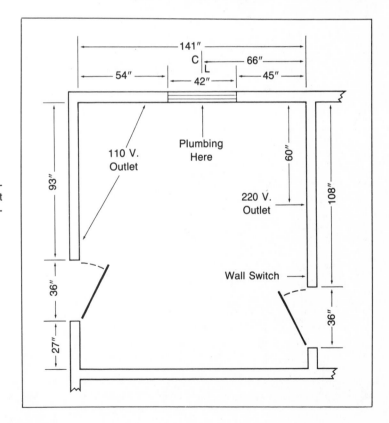

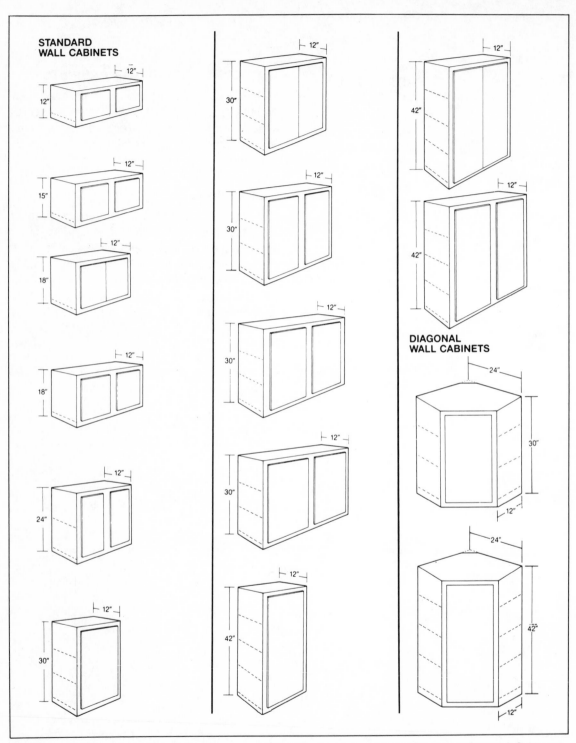

Fig. 5-6. A selection of wall cabinets offered by one manufacturer of modular cabinets (Courtesy of Scheirich Cabinetry).

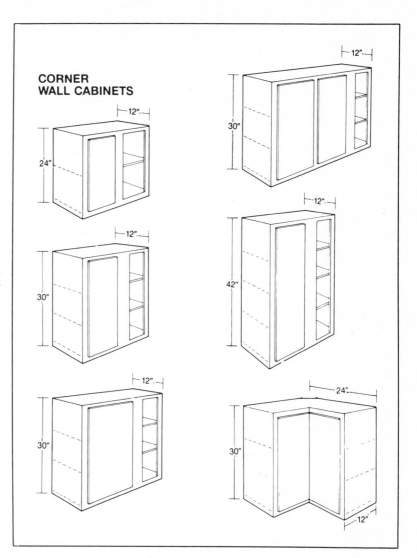

CORNER WALL CABINETS

Fig. 5-7. Standard corner wall cabinets (Courtesy of Scheirich Cabinetry).

for over refrigerators), 18 (standard for over ranges), 21, and 24 inches. Some manufacturers also offer a 24-inch deep unit specifically for use over the refrigerator.

Wall Cabinets

Wall cabinets usually come with reversible doors, or the entire cabinet can be inverted so that the door will be a left- or right-hand swing, as needed. Some have fixed shelves, some have adjustable shelves, depending on the manufacturer. There are several variations of the upper cabinet:

☐ Angle wall, or diagonal wall (Fig. 5-6): Used for turning a corner or ending a wall run at a corner, the angle wall unit has a single door at a 45 degree angle to both sides, making the interior of the cabinet more accessible. Some types have revolving lazy susan shelves, either factory installed or as an add-on option.

☐ Corner wall (Fig. 5-7): This is a 12-inch deep wall cabinet with one door on one half of the front and a blank panel on the other half. It is placed in the corner so that an adjacent run intersects and covers the blank panel. Corner cabinets can be pulled away from the wall up to about 4 inches to extend the run and make up odd inches without adding fillers.

☐ Peninsula (Fig. 5-8): This is a ceiling hung cabinet with doors on both sides, allowing access from both the kitchen and an adjacent room.

☐ Microwave (Fig. 5-8): This is a special wall cabinet designed to hold a microwave oven. Dimensions vary, but the opening in the face is usually fairly small, with a wide wooden faceframe. The faceframe can then be cut to enlarge the opening to fit your specific microwave. Microwave cabinets are usually hung beneath a standard 21-, 24-, or 30-inch cabinet to provide the correct height.

Base Cabinets

Base cabinets rest on the floor and against the wall, and form both the lower storage areas and a base for the countertops (Fig. 5-9). Base cabinets are typically 24 inches deep, and 34½ inches high, giving a finished counter height of approximately 36 inches. Widths commonly range from 12 inches to 48 inches wide in 3-inch increments (a 9-inch wide tray-base cabinet is also commonly available). All have a built-in toe space of approximately 3 × 3 inches, and are usually arranged with drawers above the doors. Some common base cabinet variations include:

☐ Sink base (Fig. 5-9): This cabinet is specifically designed for placement where the sink will sit. To allow clearance for the sink and all the accompanying plumbing, it has false drawer fronts with no drawers, and does not have a shelf. Depending on the manufacturer, it may or may not have a back. When ordering a sink base cabinet, try to select one that is at least 3 inches wider than the sink to provide adequate clearance.

☐ Sink front (Fig. 5-9): A variation of the sink base, the sink front is the cabinet front only, with no bottom, sides or back. It can be attached between two adjacent cabinets to make up a sink base. Sink fronts are especially common in corner sink installations. Fit with a plywood floor, use of the sink front allows access to the entire corner with no loss of space.

☐ Drawer base or drawer bank (Fig. 5-9): This cabinet is a base cabinet with four drawers instead of a door and a drawer.

☐ Range base: This cabinet is used with a drop-in cooktop. It has false drawer fronts and usually contains a shelf.

☐ Lazy susan (Fig. 5-9): A popular base cabinet option, the lazy susan is used in a corner to connect two runs. It has no drawers, but instead contains a 2- or 3-tier revolving set of shelves. While more expensive than other corner cabinets, it makes the best use of the space.

☐ Base corner, or blind corner (Fig. 5-9): Like the wall corner, the base corner is used to connect two adjacent runs. It has a door and a blind panel, and can be pulled several inches if needed.

☐ Peninsula: This is a base cabinet with doors and a toe kick on both sides (no drawers) for use between two adjacent rooms.

Tall Units

Most tall units are 84-inch-high cabinets, designed to span the entire distance from the floor to the top of the wall cabinets (Fig. 5-10). Other heights, most commonly 66 inches, are available from some manufacturers. Widths vary from 18 to 30 inches, and they may be 12 or 24 inches deep, depending on their intended use. Some common tall units are:

☐ Oven cabinets: These 24-inch-deep cabinets are designed to hold a single or double oven, or an oven and a microwave. They usually have an opening in the front which can be enlarged to receive the oven, and have doors above the opening and doors or drawers below. Some come with a shelf for the oven to sit on, which is installed after the opening is cut to size. If a shelf is not provided by the manufacturer, one must be site fabricated.

☐ Pantry, broom, or utility cabinets: These cabinets are 12 or 24 inches deep and used for various storage purposes.

Miscellaneous

In addition to the cabinets, your manufacturer will usually offer items like matching trim, filler

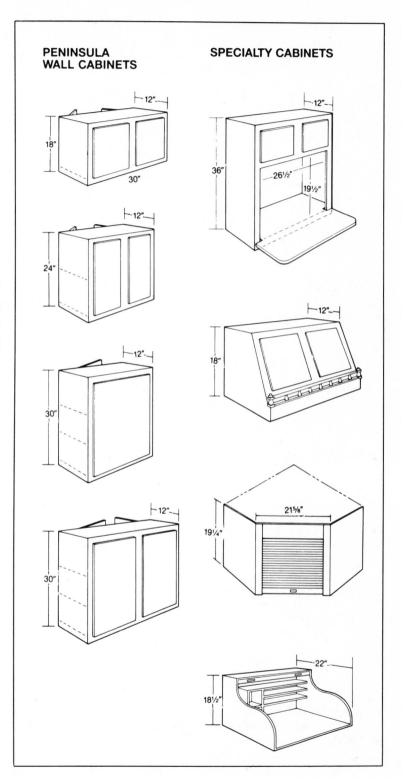

PENINSULA WALL CABINETS

SPECIALTY CABINETS

Fig. 5-8. Peninsula wall cabinets and specialty cabinets, including (right, from top) a microwave cabinet with shelf, a wooden enclosure for the range hood, an appliance garage, and a desk unit with shelves and cubbyholes (Courtesy of Scheirich Cabinetry).

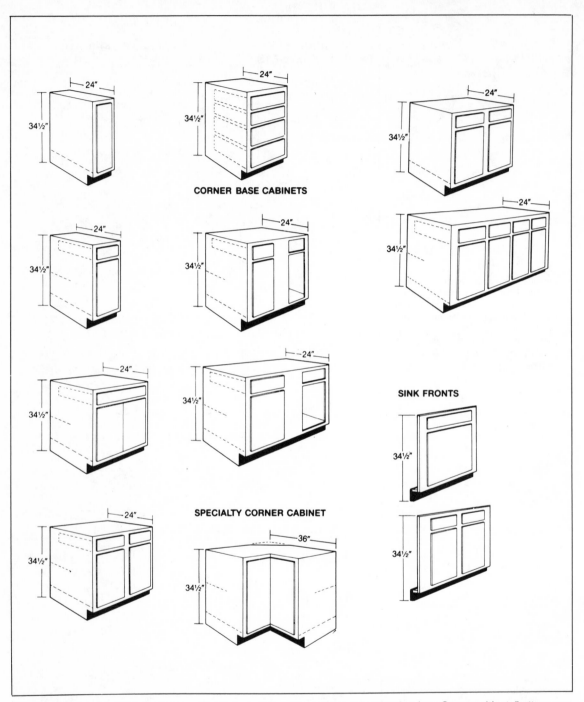

CORNER BASE CABINETS

SPECIALTY CORNER CABINET

SINK FRONTS

Fig. 5-9. A selection of standard base cabinets, including a drawer base (top center), a lazy Susan cabinet (bottom center), sink base cabinets, which are also used for the cooktop (top right) and sink fronts (bottom right) (Courtesy of Scheirich Cabinetry).

Fig. 5-10. Tall units, including oven and utility cabinets (Courtesy of Scheirich Cabinetry).

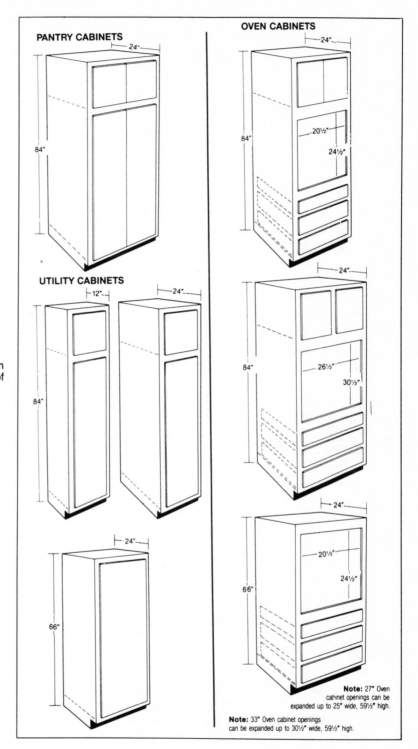

PANTRY CABINETS

24"

84"

UTILITY CABINETS

12"   24"

84"

24"

66"

OVEN CABINETS

24"

84"

20½"

24½"

24"

84"

26½"

30½"

24"

66"

20½"

24½"

Note: 27" Oven cabinet openings can be expanded up to 25" wide, 59½" high.

Note: 33" Oven cabinet openings can be expanded up to 30½" wide, 59½" high.

45

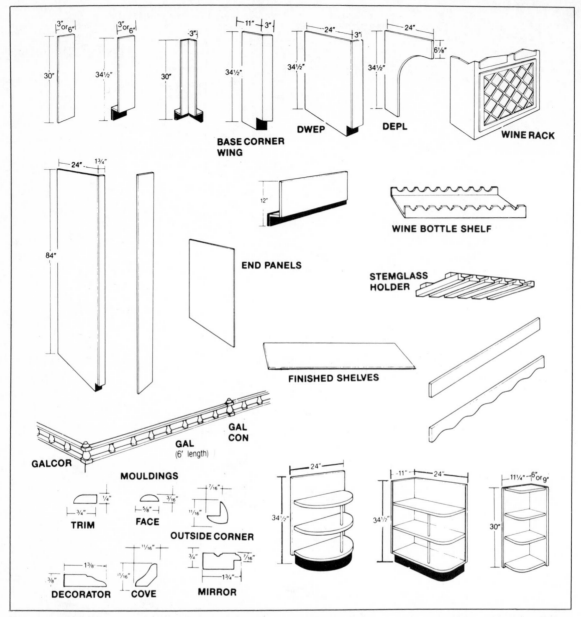

Fig. 5-11. Some fillers, trim, panels, and other miscellaneous items available to complete the modular cabinet installation. Note the ''RNG 30'' (top center), which is used to finish off between cabinets below a drop-in range (Courtesy of Scheirich Cabinetry).

strips, roll-out drawer kits, wine racks, knee-hole drawers (for use between two cabinets to create a desk), shelf kits, and other optional extras that allow you to customize your new kitchen cabinets in any manner that suits you (Fig. 5-11).

MODULAR CABINET SPECIFICATIONS

The codes used by the manufacturer to specify the cabinets may seem confusing at first, but they simply refer to the size and type of each cabinet. Understanding the specification system your manu-

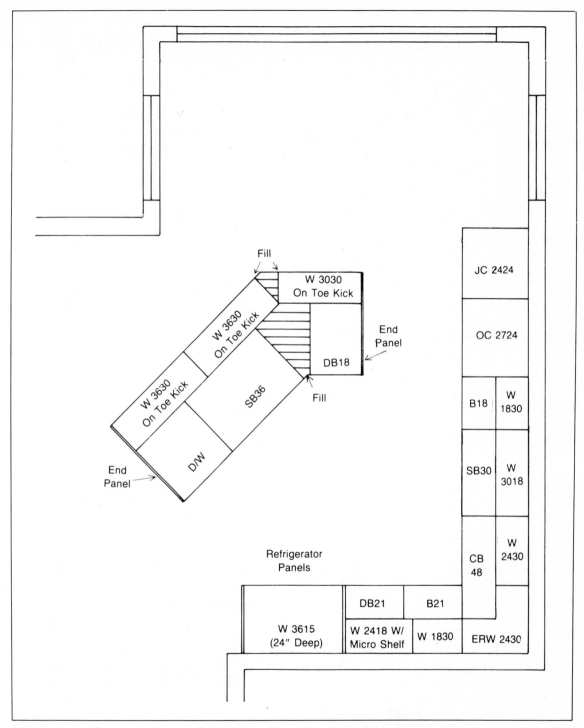

Fig. 5-12. A completed modular cabinet layout. The letters and numbers refer to the manufacturer's code numbers for the cabinets (Design courtesy of Kitchen Concepts).

facturer is using is important, both for laying out the cabinets and properly placing your order.

In general, the first number refers to the width of the cabinet and the second to the height. The letters, which may be before or after the numbers, refer to the type of cabinet. For example, a W1230 would be "W" for wall cabinet, "12" for 12 inches wide, and "30" for 30 inches high. Some manufacturers list a given height, such as 21 inches, then list widths only under that, such as W12 or W30.

Base cabinets are known to be 24 inches deep and 34½ inches high, so only the width and a letter designation are usually given. Some examples would be B24, for a 24-inch-wide base cabinet, D18 or DB18 for an 18-inch-wide drawer cabinet, and SB36 for a 36-inch-wide sink base. If the cabinet is not reversible, an "L" or "R" designation will follow the size, indicating that the cabinet is hinged on the left or the right.

COMBINING MODULAR CABINETS TO FIT YOUR KITCHEN

When you have your drawing prepared, make several good photocopies of it. This will give you plenty of copies to try different cabinet layouts on without having to continually redraw the original outlines of the room. You'll also need a manufacturer's specification guide that shows exactly what cabinets are available in what sizes.

Many designers begin with the sink, centering a sink base or sink front cabinet at that location and working out from there. Another option is to work out from each corner. In either case, what you are striving for is a sense of symmetry with the cabinets.

Using the grids on the graph paper as a guide, lay out the various cabinets to exact scale, and label each one as you go with the manufacturer's code number (Fig. 5-12). Don't be concerned if it takes you several attempts to get a workable design. Professional designers make several attempts also. These general rules will make the layout easier and more professional:

☐ Lay the base cabinets out first, since the base cabinet layout is partially dictated by the appliance layout and the work triangle. Continue

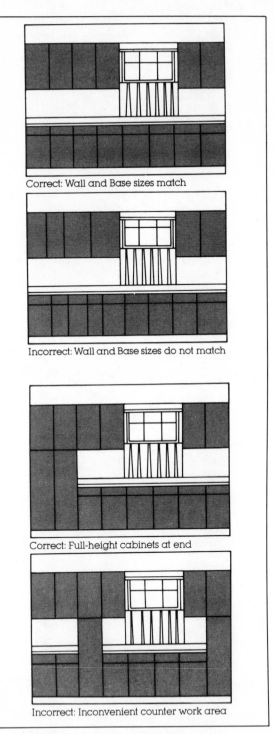

Correct: Wall and Base sizes match

Incorrect: Wall and Base sizes do not match

Correct: Full-height cabinets at end

Incorrect: Inconvenient counter work area

Fig. 5-13. Some of the do's and don'ts when laying out your cabinets (Courtesy of Kitchen Kompact).

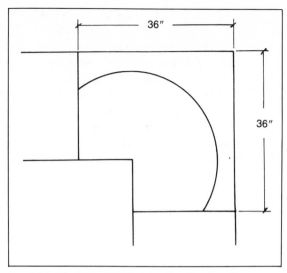

Fig. 5-14. Allow 36 inches in each direction from the corner when planning for a lazy-Susan corner cabinet.

working with them until the design is right before starting on the wall units.

☐ Upper cabinets should match lower cabinets so that the doors will be vertically aligned when the cabinets are installed (Fig. 5-13). For example, use a 30-inch-wall cabinet over a 30-inch base cabinet, or two 24-inch wall cabinets over a 48-inch base.

☐ Space should be divided equally wherever possible. For example, to fill a 60-inch space, two 30-inch cabinets will look better than using a 36 and a 24.

☐ Tall units should be placed at the end of a run, not in the middle where they will interrupt the flow of the counter space. (Fig. 5-13).

☐ When you are not using corner cabinets, fillers should be used in the corners to ensure that adequate clearance is provided to open the drawers.

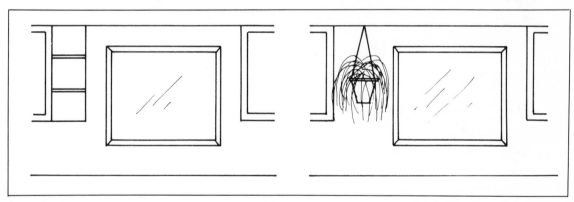

Fig. 5-15. Using shelves (left) and a hanging plant to balance off an uneven reveal next to a window.

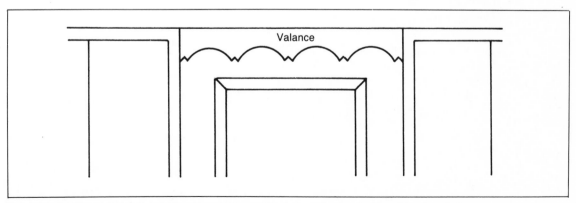

Fig. 5-16. A valance board is usually used to connect the two cabinets on either side of a window.

- [ ] If fill pieces are necessary to make up for odd inches, they should be placed in the corners rather than in the middle of the run to avoid throwing the base cabinets off from the uppers. Also, divide the fills as evenly as possible, rather than placing them all in one location.
- [ ] Lazy-Susan cabinets usually require a full 36 inches of space from each corner (Fig. 5-14). Blind corner cabinets can be pulled to make up odd inches without fills.
- [ ] Try to make the space on each side of a window equal, if possible. If a large space is present on one side and a small space on the other, consider shelves or perhaps a hanging plant on the large side to balance things out (Fig. 5-15).
- [ ] The open space between cabinets on either side of a window is normally spanned by using a valance (Fig. 5-16). Most manufacturers offer decorative valance material to match the cabinets.

Chapter 6

Bright Ideas for Lighting

PROPER LIGHTING HAS LONG BEEN ESTABLISHED as being essential to safety, good health, and a general feeling of well-being (Fig. 6-1). The need for effective lighting is at its greatest in the kitchen, where meal preparation, entertaining, and a variety of other tasks all require proper levels of illumination (Table 6-1).

You'll want to establish a good, workable lighting plan early. This allows for the proper placement of wiring, fixture boxes, and switches as the kitchen is being worked on. Good lighting stems from good planning—it should never be an afterthought.

INCANDESCENT VS. FLUORESCENT LIGHT

Incandescent light is produced by passing an electric current through a tungsten filament (Fig. 6-2) causing the filament to glow and give off light. The resulting light is warm and yellow, and is generally preferred by most people. Incandescent light also consumes more electricity, produces more shadows, and gives off heat.

Fluorescent light (Fig. 6-2), on the other hand, is created when electrons are given off by an electric arc inside the tube. The electrons combine with mercury to create ultraviolet rays, which then react with the tube's phosphorescent coating to produce visible light. Fluorescent tubes last about 5 to

10 times as long as incandescent bulbs, use about one-third the electricity, and produce virtually shadow-free light over a wide area.

The big disadvantage to fluorescent light for most people is the cold, bluish tint it gives off. There are, however, several shades of light available in fluorescent tubes, so this problem is easily overcome. Warm white tubes give off a yellowish light similar to incandescent and is flattering to people and food. Deluxe cool white tubes give accurate color renditions, which might be important in a colorfully decorated kitchen, and blends well with cool colors.

In most kitchens, designers combine incandescent and fluorescent lights to create good lighting patterns in a mood that's compatible with the overall kitchen design.

MEASURING LIGHT

The basic unit of light intensity is the *footcandle*. This is the amount of light that a standard candle would throw onto an object that is one foot away.

Light from a given light source is measured in *lumens*, which is the basic unit of light quantity. Lumens are a more common term in everyday use than footcandles, and the rating of a bulb or tube in lumens is usually given on the manufacturer's package. A candle, for example, produces about 12

Table 6-1. Kitchen Lighting Guidelines.

Kitchen Areas	Fixture Placement	Incandescent Lamping	Fluorescent Lamping
Counter lighting	Under cabinets: mount fluorescent fixtures as close to the front of the cabinet as possible		Tubes long enough to extend ⅔ length of counter; e.g., 36″ 30W or 48″ 40W
	Counters with no overhead cabinets: hang pendant 24″-27″ above the counter OR	60-75W for every 20 inches of counter	Same as above
	Recessed or surface mounted units: 16″-24″ apart, centered over the counter	75W reflector lamp	2-tube fixture extending ⅔ length of counter
At the range	Built-in hood light	60W bulb	
	With no hood, place recessed or surface mounted units 15″-18″ apart over the center of the range	Minimum of 2 75W reflector floods	2 36″ 30W or 3 24″ 20W
At the sink	Same as for range	Same as for range	Same as for range
Eating area	Pendant centered 30″ above table or counter; multiple pendants over counters 4′ or longer	1 100W or 2 60W or 3 40W or 50/100/150W	

Placement and minimum lamping guidelines for the kitchen.
Lamping refers to the bulb or tube source of light used in a fixture
Pendant is a hanging fixture smaller than a chandelier
(Courtesy of the American Home Lighting Institute)

lumens of light; a new 75-watt incandescent bulb produces about 1,180, and a new 40-watt warm white fluorescent tube about 3,150.

GENERAL LIGHTING

There are three types of lighting; general, task, and accent or decorative. Quite often, you will find a combination of all three in a well-lighted kitchen.

General lighting provides a comfortable, overall level of light for the room or area, allowing you to see and move about safely. General lighting is usually accomplished with the use of ceiling-mounted fixtures or luminous ceiling panels, centered or equally spaced in the room.

The size of the fixture should relate to the size of the area. If you are using fluorescent light, plan on providing about ¾ to 1 watt per square foot of floor area. For incandescent light, use about 1½ to 2 watts per square foot.

Offset track or shielded fluorescent lights work well for general lighting also. They should be ceiling mounted about 18 to 24 inches from the cabinets, and arranged in a pattern that suits the space being illuminated.

Fig. 6-1. Adequate lighting in the proper layout is essential for a bright, cheerful, and efficient kitchen (Courtesy of the American Home Lighting Institute).

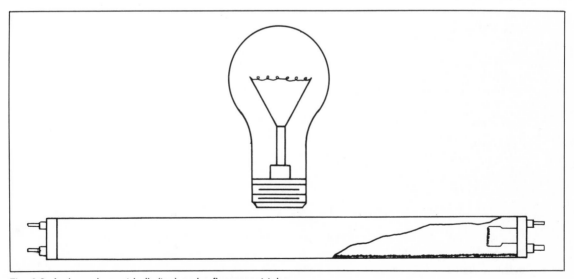

Fig. 6-2. An incandescent bulb (top) and a fluorescent tube.

53

If there is a dining area, a chandelier hung over the table usually adds to the level of general lighting in the room. The size of the chandelier, as a general rule of thumb, should be in inches what the diagonal of the room area is in feet. It should not, however, be greater than the width of the table minus 12 inches, to prevent people from hitting their heads.

Downlights, which direct their light down instead of all around as a chandelier does, can provide intimate general lighting over the eating area also. For this application, 65- or 75-watt PAR floodlight bulbs are common.

Luminous Ceilings

Known by a variety of names, the luminous ceiling is an easy effect to create and construct. It provides excellent, unobtrusive general lighting, blends nicely with the kitchen decor, and is usually inexpensive when compared with the cost of individual light fixtures (Fig. 6-3).

In general, the luminous ceiling is created by first constructing a recess in the ceiling (Fig. 6-4). This recess might be a boxed opening made by cutting and spanning the ceiling joists with headers, or it might be no more than just openings between the joists or trusses. Fluorescent fixtures are then placed in the recesses, following the watts per square foot formula given earlier.

To finish off the luminous ceiling, translucent plastic panels, called diffusers, are used. Diffuser panels come in a variety of textures and tones, and are usually 2 × 4 or 4 × 4 feet in size. To support the panels, an appropriate sized grid of wood is created, stained to match the cabinets. The wooden grid is attached flat against the ceiling, and the diffusers are slipped into place. Removal of the diffusers also gives access for changing the tubes.

If desired, thin metal channels can be used to create the grid. These can then be painted the same color as the ceiling to blend them in, or a contrasting color to make them stand out as an accent.

Light Boxes

A variation of the luminous ceiling is the light box (Fig. 6-5). Here, a box takes the place of the recess in the ceiling. The light box stands out more than the luminous ceiling and is usually more expensive to construct, but it works well when construction details make building the recess impractical or undesirable. The light box can also be hung from the ceiling on chains, offering an ideal solution to the problems of lighting a kitchen with a vaulted ceiling.

The box should be constructed out of lumber or plywood that matches the kitchen cabinetry. It is built with four sides, a completely or partially solid top, and an open bottom. On the bottom, a grid is created with lumber or moldings that will hold the diffusers. Remember that the box will need to be deep enough to house the fixtures and tubes, and still allow the diffusers to be inserted and removed.

To mount the box, screw through the top into the ceiling joists, or use eye bolts and chain. If the box is chain mounted, you can weave the electrical wire through the chain and into the box, making it less visible. Several styles of already constructed light boxes are also available (Fig. 6-6).

TASK LIGHTING

Task lighting is provided in addition to general lighting to illuminate specific work areas, such as counters, cooking equipment, etc. (Fig. 6-7). It should provide adequate, fairly concentrated light that is glare- and shadow-free. To protect against glare, the amount of general lighting should be more than one-third of the light supplied by the task lights.

In the kitchen, task lighting should be provided over the sink for cleanup chores, over the cooktop for meal preparation, and under the cabinets to illuminate the countertops. Range hoods normally come with a light as part of the unit to provide light over the cooktop. If using a downdraft cooktop with no hood, plan on installing some sort of fixture under the cabinet above the cooktop.

Individual task lighting should also be provided for a separate desk, meal planning area, or other work center. For islands, consider a hanging pendant lamp in addition to the illumination provided from the general lighting.

For undercabinet lights, a standard rule of thumb is to use a fixture or fixtures equal to two-thirds the length of the counter (Fig. 6-8). The fixture should be placed as close to the front of the

e joists and

itchen and
: one wall,
n each ob-
ected up,
ts or the
vay of il-
ets is to
or clear
ontrolled

her glass
cabinet.
f a small

even, unobtrusive light in this kitchen (Courtesy of Lightolier).

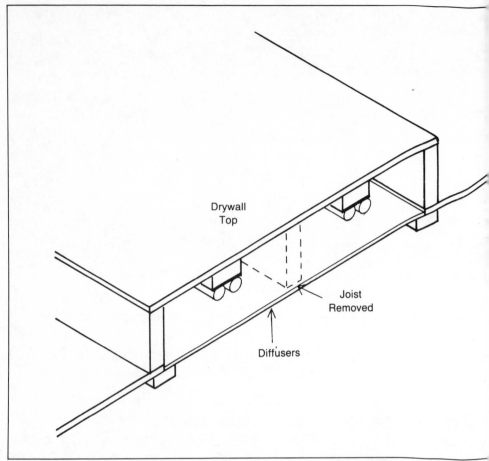

Drywall
Top

Joist
Removed

Diffusers

Fig. 6-4. Construction details for a luminous ceiling. In typical construction, an area is boxed in betw covered with drywall, then finished off with a wooden or metal faceframe and diffusers.

cabinet as possible, and shielded from view. A valance built from wood that matches the cabinet can be attached to the bottom of the cabinet to conceal the fixture. Try to provide one 20-watt tube for every 3 feet of counter space.

ACCENT OR DECORATIVE LIGHTING

Accent or decorative lighting is lighting that is used to highlight or accent a specific object or area, such as a painting, a plant, or even an entire wall. Accent lighting is bright and concentrated, usually about three times as bright as the general light falling on the accented object.

Accented areas are a matter of personal taste,

and depend largely on the layout o its contents. If you have art object a track light with small, individual s ject might be just right. Soffit ligh can illuminate the area above the walls up to a vaulted ceiling. An luminating the objects on top of th lay a concealed string of small Christmas lights on top of the cab by a switch.

If you have a china cabinet, hut fronted cabinets, consider a light in This illuminates the contents, and t amount of reflected light.

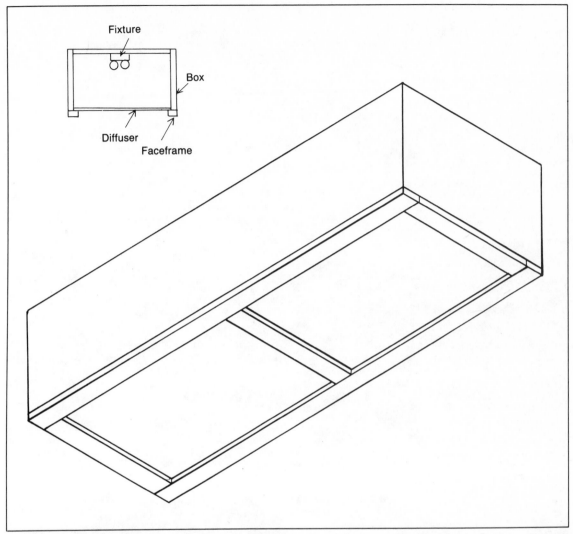

Fixture

Box

Diffuser

Faceframe

Fig. 6-5. An easily built light box for mounting directly on the ceiling. This type of box can also be hung on chains for lighting a kitchen with high ceilings.

SWITCHING

An important consideration in your lighting plan is the switching layout (Fig. 6-9). Multiple switches are highly recommended by most designers over having one switch control the entire kitchen. Multiple switching offers energy savings and better control over the lighting.

Consider the following guidelines for switches, and adapt them as necessary to your lighting plan:

☐ In general, ceiling mounted lighting should be on one switch. If the kitchen is large, divide the lighting load equally and place on two switches.

☐ A light over an eating area should be switched separately from the other general lighting. If the light is incandescent, consider placing it on a dimmer switch for energy saving and better control of the light levels. (Some types of fluorescent lights can also be placed on dimmers—check with

57

Fig. 6-6. An attractive manufactured fluorescent light box which compliments the cabinets. Note the small task lights under the wall cabinets (Courtesy of Lightolier).

Fig. 6-7. Effective task lighting over a serving counter (right) and used as accent lighting (Courtesy of Lightolier).

Fig. 6-8. Undercabinet lighting should equal approximately two-thirds of the length of the counter it's illuminating.

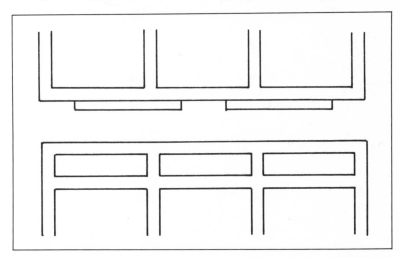

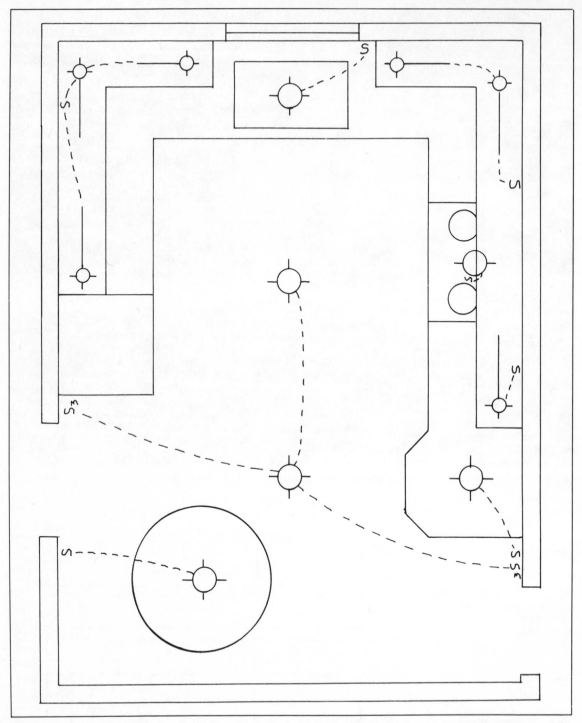

Fig. 6-9. A well-thought-out lighting and switch plan. Note the separate switching for general and task lighting, and the three-way switches at the two entrances.

the manufacturer for specific recommendations.)

☐ The lights over the sink, cooktop, desk, and island should each have a separate switch. Dimmer switches on desk and island lights allow them to be used as mood or background lighting.

☐ Undercabinet lights should be on at least two switches, with each switch controlling half the lights. If you have a number of separate work areas that are lit by undercabinet lights, place the light(s) for each work area on a separate switch.

☐ Switch accent lights separately from other lights, and consider placing track or other incandescent accent lights on a dimmer control.

☐ Group the general lighting switches together in a convenient location, and place each of the task and accent light switches at the point of use.

☐ If your kitchen has a natural traffic pattern through it, place the general lighting on 3- or 4-way switches. This placement of switches makes it convenient to turn the lights on as you enter the room and off as you leave, without a lot of backtracking. The rule of thumb is that if the room has entrances located more than 10 feet apart, each entrance should have a switch.

Chapter 7

Removing the Old Kitchen

BEFORE CONSTRUCTION CAN BEGIN ON THE NEW kitchen, the old one must be removed. This is not a particularly difficult task, but there are some procedures to follow that will make it safer, and that will make the later patching in a lot easier.

The main thing to remember is to work slowly and carefully. The goal is to remove the old kitchen with as little damage to the surrounding areas as possible, to minimize reconstruction work. Always know exactly what you're about to remove, and plan each step carefully to minimize the risk. Many of the objects you'll be handling are heavy and awkward, so you'll need to have a helper available to lend a hand.

GETTING READY

There isn't anything that disrupts the running of the household more than the removal of the kitchen. Cooking and cleaning facilities are in disarray; food and utensils are not within reach. The entire hub of the home is temporarily out of action.

You will be without a kitchen for a period of several days up to several weeks. If you are using an experienced contractor, the disruption period will be kept to a minimum. If you're doing the work yourself, the time frame could be considerably longer. In either case, preparing yourself, mentally as well as physically, will go a long way toward easing the strain on you and the family.

Several days before the dismanteling begins, begin preparing a temporary kitchen. This temporary kitchen might be in the dining room, in the den, or in any convenient room. Set up folding tables or sheets of plywood on boxes to serve as temporary counterspace, and lay in a supply of paper plates, paper and foam cups, and plastic utensils to keep dishwashing at a minimum.

For cooking facilities, a microwave oven is a great help. If you don't have one but are purchasing one for the new kitchen, arrange for it to be delivered early so you can begin using it. A hotplate will work well for most cooking chores, as will a portable electric fry pan or griddle. A propane powered campstove will work in a pinch; be certain you provide adequate ventilation, and be careful with the open flame. Move your refrigerator into your temporary kitchen, or at least have it nearby.

Begin emptying out the cabinets systematically. This systematic approach will keep you organized in your temporary kitchen, and will make moving into the new kitchen a lot easier. Start by boxing up all the nonessential items, such as special china and silver, holiday dishes, etc. Label each box, and store them in the garage or other out of the way place.

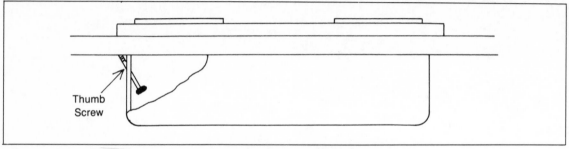

Fig. 7-1. The typical location of the thumbscrews that hold a cooktop in place.

Pack up appliances, utensils, dishes, and other everyday items that you won't be using for the time being, and store those in the garage also. Keep a few sizes of mixing bowls out, and a minimum number of utensils. Also keep microwave bowls and dishes handy.

Finally, pack the food. Arrange it in boxes in roughly the same way it was in the cabinets, to make finding things easier. Sturdy cardboard or wooden boxes, placed on their sides in your temporary kitchen, make good temporary cabinets. Keep those food items you know you'll be using in the front, within easy reach.

By the day you or the contractors are ready to begin the tear-out, the entire kitchen should be empty. Don't expect the contractors to empty it out for you—in most cases you'll be charged extra for their time.

REMOVING APPLIANCES AND FIXTURES

The kitchen is dismantled in the opposite order in which it was first assembled, so the first things to come out are the appliances and fixtures. Before you start, locate the water and gas shutoffs, and the electrical service panel. Next, set aside an area in the garage or side yard for all the debris. If you intend to save, recycle, or sell any of the items removed from the kitchen, be sure they're protected from the weather.

Locate the circuit breakers for each of the appliances and shut them off. Be sure and test each appliance individually to verify that the electricity is off before you begin working on it. Shut off the gas at the fixture supply or at the main, and shut off the water to the sink and dishwasher, either at the shutoffs under the sink or at the main shutoff valve. Verify that the water and gas are off before proceeding.

Removing the Appliances

Most appliances are installed in roughly the same manner, although there may be some variations from brand to brand. Refer to the general instructions given below, then study the actual appliance carefully before proceeding. If you have access to the original instruction book that came with the appliance, installation instructions are usually provided. Simply reverse those installation instructions to remove the unit.

☐ Ranges: Drop-in ranges may be resting on feet on the floor, on a cabinet shelf, or simply hanging from the edges of the countertop. First, open the oven door and study the vertical edges of the oven. Remove any screws that go through the oven into the cabinet. Next, lift up the lid around the burners, and remove any screws or thumbscrews that are securing the unit against the counter.

With a helper, slide the unit out of the opening and set it on the floor. You will find either a gas line or a flexible metal electrical cable. Trace it back to the gas valve or junction box where it's connected, and remove it.

If the range is freestanding, it will be plugged into a large wall socket. Simply slide the unit away from the wall, then locate and remove the plug.

☐ Cooktops: A drop-in cooktop is usually held in place with two or more thumbscrews (Fig. 7-1).

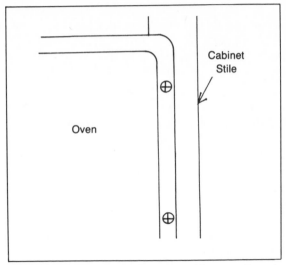

Fig. 7-2. A built-in oven is held in place with screws through the frame into the cabinet's stiles.

If the unit has a lid that lifts up, they'll usually be located inside, at the two side edges. If there is no lid, look up inside the cabinet, against the bottom of the countertop.

Loosen the screws until they swing out of the way, or remove them completely. Discon-

nect the power cable or gas line, and remove the unit.

☐ Ovens: Ovens are attached with four or more flathead screws that are driven through the front of the oven case (Fig. 7-2), on either side of the oven cavity, into the surrounding wood of the cabinets. Remove the screws, and slide the unit out far enough to get access to the power cable or gas line. Disconnect the line, then with a helper, remove the oven.

Removing the Plumbing

☐ Dishwasher: A dishwasher has three lines attached to it; water supply, drain, and electrical (Fig. 7-3). You'll need to locate each one and disconnect or cut it first, before the dishwasher can be removed.

First, remove the screws that hold the bottom front panel in place (below the main door). The screws are located on the sides of the panel, on the front, or on the top and bottom. With the panel removed, you should see the water supply line, which is usually a copper tube that runs to the hot water valve under the sink. Disconnect the fitting that holds the tube in place.

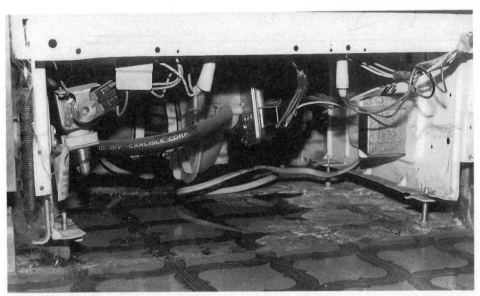

Fig. 7-3. Removing the dishwasher requires disconnecting the water supply (valve at left), the drain line (black hose in center), and the electrical wiring (in metal junction box at right).

The drain fitting is a rubber hose, connected to the bottom of the dishwasher and to the air gap, the garbage disposal, or the drain pipe under the sink. Disconnect or cut it at any convenient spot. Finally, you'll find the electrical cable connected to a junction box under the dishwasher. Remove the box lid, and disconnect the cable.

The dishwasher itself is held in place by two screws at the top of the tub, driven through brackets into the underside of the countertop. Remove the screws, and the entire unit should slide out. If it doesn't, you may have to lower the leveling feet on the bottom to get it to drop down sufficiently for removal.

☐ Garbage Disposal: To remove the garbage disposal, first disconnect the electrical cable. This may be simply plugged into a wall socket, or it may need to be disconnected at the junction box on the wall or on the unit. Disconnect the main drain line and, if applicable, the rubber drain line from the dishwasher.

The garbage disposal is attached to a metal fitting on the bottom of the sink by means of a metal ring. Rotating the ring about half a turn from right to left will loosen the unit and allow you to remove it. You may need to use a screwdriver or a hammer to tap the fitting loose. Some models are held in place with three screws, so if you can't locate the ring, look for the screws.

☐ Sink: The first step is to remove the plumbing under the sink, either by disconnecting the fittings or cutting the lines. You'll need to disconnect the hot and cold water lines, and the drain lines and trap. Don't worry about removing the faucet, that will come off with the sink.

The sink itself is held in by one of four methods. Study it carefully and see which one seems likely for yours:

Stainless steel sinks: Stainless steel sinks have a channel welded to the underside of the sink rim, with clips and screws that hold the sink tight against the counter. Loosen the screws and remove or swing the clips aside, then pry up the sink.

Sinks with sink rims: These sinks are similar to stainless steel, except that the rim is a separate piece. The screws and clips hold the sink, the rim, and the counter all sandwiched together. Simply remove the screws and clips.

Self-rimming: These sinks are fairly new, and are usually heavy, cast iron sinks. Self-rimming sinks have a smooth, rounded edge, and no sink rim. Nothing holds them in place except a bead of sealant between the underside of the sink rim and the counter, plus their own weight. To remove them, just pry up.

Tiled-in: Many sinks are set on the countertop decking and then held in place with tile. You will need to chip off the old tile to completely expose the rim of the sink, then pry the sink up.

REMOVING THE CABINETS

The next step in the demolition of the kitchen is to remove the cabinets. You'll want to exercise care in removing them so that they come down intact. They are easier to handle that way, and used kitchen cabinets almost always have some value. They are great for use in the garage or basement, or even in a family room or the kitchen of your summer cabin. You might even be able to sell them to someone else who has a similar use for them.

It's usually easiest to remove the upper cabinets first. Start by unscrewing and removing the doors (Fig. 7-4), which makes the cabinets lighter and easier to handle. If you intend to salvage the cabinets, number the doors so they can be put back in the same order.

Study the inside of the case and look for where the cabinets are joined to the wall and to each other. If the cabinets are modular, you'll find they are screwed together through the edges of the face frame. These should be the first screws to be removed. Remove the screws that hold the cabinets to the wall next, having a helper brace the cabinet while you remove the screws. Ease the cabinet down the wall until it rests on the counter, then lift it and remove it to an out of the way area.

In some instances, nails are used instead of screws. Use a cat claw (Fig. 7-5) or other type of nail puller to get under the head and raise the nail, then remove it with a hammer. Use a block of wood under the hammer head if extra leverage is needed. If you can't get a puller under the nail head, you may have to resort to working a wrecking bar in behind the cabinets and prying them off the wall. Use care to avoid damage to both the cabinets and the surface of the wall.

When all of the upper cabinets have been removed, the countertops are the next step. If the counters are plastic laminate, they can be removed in one piece, and even reused on the new cabinets if desired. You'll usually find that screws have been driven up through cleats on the top of the base cabi-nets, into the underside of the counters. To free up the counters, simply remove the screws.

If the counters are L- or U-shaped, you'll probably find special threaded bolts holding the corner joints together. After you remove the screws from the cabinets, tip the counters up until the corner bolts are exposed, and loosen them with a wrench and remove them. Carefully separate the counters along the joint, which is usually glued for extra strength.

Tile counters usually need to be broken up to be removed, especially if they have a mortar base. Glazed tile can be razor sharp when cracked, and you'll find sharp wire embedded in the mortar. Also,

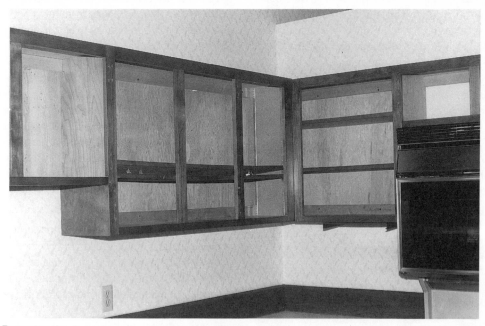

Fig. 7-4. Removing the doors from the cabinets will make them lighter and easier to handle. Number them so they can be put back on in order.

Fig. 7-5. A "cat claw" nail puller. The sharpened, slotted head is driven under the head of the nail, then levered back to pull the nail (Courtesy of Stanley Tools).

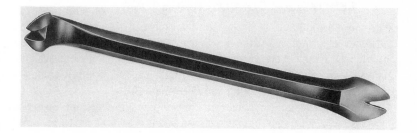

67

the mortar and tile fragments will chip off into small, sharp pieces and fly everywhere. Wear goggles and heavy gloves during any tile breaking operations.

Working from the front, use a hammer and break off the edge cap. If you can, drive a wrecking bar under the mortar base and pry up the counter in sections. In some cases, all or most of the counter might come up at once, and you'll need to use a heavy hammer to break it into sections that are small enough to carry. Fill up small, heavy cardboard boxes with the broken tile, making it easier to carry and dispose of.

When the counters have been removed, the base cabinets can be taken out. Unscrew them as you did with the upper cabinets; remove the doors, take out the screws from the faceframe, then remove the screws from the wall. In some instances, the cabinets will also be toenailed into the floor, necessitating the use of a wrecking bar to pry them up.

Some older styles of cabinets were site-built in place by the carpenters who constructed the house. These cabinets often have no backs. They are merely shelves supported on wall cleats with a faceframe and some doors. If you've determined that your kitchen has this type of cabinet, little can be done to salvage them.

Begin by unscrewing and removing the doors. Using a hammer from the inside of the cabinet, knock the faceframe free of the shelves. Depending on how the cabinets were originally built, you can then either remove the sides to completely free up the shelves, or pry the entire cabinet off the wall or off the cleats. Remember to wear goggles and gloves, as these types of cabinets were usually assembled with a great number of finishing nails.

REMOVING FLOORCOVERINGS

With any new kitchen, replacing the flooring is almost inevitable. Rarely will the new cabinets go back exactly where the old ones came out, and it's usually impossible to patch old floorcoverings. With the cabinets out, study the old flooring and determine the best way to proceed.

If the old flooring is tile or linoleum and it's in good condition and well adhered to the floor, you can probably lay the new flooring right over it. If the old floor's at all in bad shape, however, you'll get a better finished product by removing it.

In some instances, the cabinets were installed first, followed by underlayment and then flooring. If this was the case, you'll find large gaps in the underlayment when the cabinets are removed. Your best bet here, rather than patching in the underlayment, is to simply remove it, flooring and all.

If you intend to leave the existing underlayment and remove the floorcovering, you'll need to get under it and carefully scrape it up. Hand scrapers such as a stiff putty knife or wide chisel will work, but it's tedious work. Long-handled floor scrapers will save some wear and tear on your back, or you can rent electric floor scrapers from most rental yards. The electric models work well on some types of flooring, but not all—discuss the details with your rental dealer to see what he thinks.

Kitchen carpeting is almost always glued down. If the carpeting has a regular back, it can usually be pulled up leaving only a residue of glue that can be scraped or sanded off. If the carpet has a foam back, pulling it up will leave a considerable amount of foam stuck to the floor. You'll need to scrape this off completely to prepare for the new flooring.

Other Tear-out

When the room has been stripped of the appliances, cabinets, countertops, and flooring, study the proposed layout to see what else needs to be removed. It's best to completely prepare the room at one time, avoiding delays and additional mess down the road.

If the walls need to be opened up to provide access for new plumbing or wiring, get as much of this out of the way now as possible. Locate the studs on either side of the area you need to tear into, and cut down the center of the studs with a utility knife or a reciprocating saw. A little extra time spent making clean wall cutouts will save you hours of work when it comes time to patch everything up again.

As a final tear-out step, completely clean the kitchen. Sweep up all the debris, and remove everything to an out of the way storage area for later disposal.

Chapter 8

Plumbing Techniques

MOST KITCHEN REMODELS WILL INVOLVE SOME reworking of the existing plumbing. This rework might be as simple as adding an icemaker line for the new refrigerator, or as involved as moving the sink to a new location. The fittings and pipe used by today's plumbers have simplified these tasks immensely, and many of the plumbing tasks you'll encounter in the kitchen can be handled by any patient do-it-yourselfer.

There are two basic plumbing systems at work in the kitchen—water supply, and drain, waste and vent (DWV). In general, water is supplied to the house through a main line, which is regulated by a main shutoff valve. This line branches off to supply cold water to the various fixtures and faucets in the home, and also supplies cold water to the water heater. The water heater warms the water to around 120 to 140 degrees, then supplies it to the faucets through a separate set of lines.

Drain lines carry off liquid waste, such as that from the shower, the washing machine, or the bathroom sink. Waste lines, also called soil lines, carry both liquid and solid waste, as from the kitchen sink or the toilet. The lines tie together and empty into the house sewer line, which carries the waste away from the house for disposal in the sewer system or septic system. Vent lines, rising through the roof of the house, carry off sewer gasses and equalize the pressure in the system to keep it flowing.

Water lines, being pressurized, can be added to and extended to new locations fairly easily. Drain and waste lines, on the other hand, need to slope from the point of origin to the point of disposal, allowing the waste in them to move by gravity. When extending or altering a drain or waste line, it is necessary to keep this basic principle in mind. This slope, called the "fall" of the pipe, should be maintained at approximately ¼ inch per foot. If it's much less than that, the water will not flow; too much more than that and the liquid waste will run out faster than the solids, causing clogged pipes.

PIPE AND FITTINGS

Today's well-equipped plumbing supply store offers quite a variety of pipes and fittings, many of which are inexpensive and easy to work with. Look over the choices carefully, compare the fittings and assembly methods, and select a material that you feel comfortable working with.

The most common materials you will encounter in older homes are galvanized metal pipe for the water lines, and cast iron pipe for the DWV system.

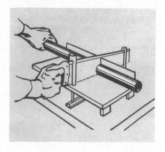

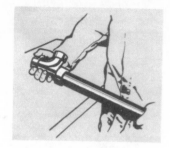

1. Cut pipe square. Use saw and mitre box or plastic tube cutter. Remove all burrs from both the inside and outside of the pipe with a knife, file or reamer. Remove dirt, grease and moisture. A thorough wipe with a clean dry rag is usually sufficient. Check dry fit. For proper interference fit, pipe should go easily into fitting ¼ to ¾ of the way.

2. Using a suitable applicator, apply a moderate even coat of cement to the fitting socket. (Care should be taken not to allow solvent cement to puddle in fitting socket.) Apply a liberal coat of cement to the pipe equal to the depth of the fitting socket. Cement must be applied in sufficient quantities to fill the joint.

3. Without delay, assemble while cement is still wet. Use sufficient force to insure that pipe bottoms in socket. If possible, twist the pipe or fitting ⅛ to ¼ turn as assembled. Hold together about 30 seconds to make sure joint does not separate. With a rag, wipe off excess cement. Avoid disturbing the joint.

Fig. 8-1. The proper techniques for working with ABS plastic pipe and fittings (Courtesy of Nibco, Inc.).

Both materials are used far less frequently today as newer, easier to use materials have come on the market. Transition fittings, covered in more detail below, make it possible to easily go from whatever material was originally used in your home to any of the newer materials you choose to use.

ABS Pipe

The most common choice for DWV lines in today's construction is pipe and fittings made from acrylonitrile-butadiene-styrene, a black plastic material known simply as ABS. Common pipe sizes are 1½, 2, 3, and 4 inches, and there are a wide variety of compatible fittings available. The pipe is sold in 20-foot lengths, or you can buy cut lengths by the foot at most dealers.

ABS is a very simple material to work with (Fig. 8-1). The pipe can be cut with any fine-toothed handsaw, or a hacksaw will work. Care must be taken to cut the pipe square, not at an angle. This ensures full contact with the inner shoulder of the fitting, and makes for a good joint. If desired, you can use a backsaw in a miter box to make quick cuts that are perfectly square. After making the cut, use a small rasp or knife to remove any burrs and smooth the cut edge.

The pipe and fittings are joined using a liquid solvent cement. A small dabber is included in the can, which makes application of the cement easy and convenient. When assembling ABS pipe, first cut the pipe to length and test fit it with the proper fittings in place. This step is important, because the glue joint, once made, cannot be undone. If you've made a mistake with the finished joint, the fitting must be cut out and discarded.

Using the dabber in the can, apply an even, liberal coat of cement to the outside of the pipe. Make sure there are no dry spots on the pipe, and that it is coated to the full depth that it will penetrate into the fitting. Apply a thin, even coat to the inside of the socket. Insert the pipe into the fitting with a slight twisting motion until the pipe has seated completely into the socket on the fitting, then align the fitting so it is pointing correctly. Remember to twist and then align the fitting quickly, as the cement will set within just a few seconds.

PVC Pipe

Another fairly common choice for DWV systems is polyvinyl chloride (PVC), and in some instances PVC and ABS are used together in the same system. If you are combining fittings of one material with pipe of another material, make certain you use a cement that is compatible with both.

There are different schedules of PVC pipe, which refers to the thickness of the pipe wall and, in turn, the pipe's pressure rating. Thick-walled schedule 40 pipe is the most common for use in DWV systems, and most fittings you find will be manufactured from schedule 40 material. PVC pipe is joined with a liquid solvent cement, and is cut and worked using the same tools and methods as are used for ABS.

Copper Pipe

For water lines, corrosion-resistant copper pipe is still the most widely used material. It is light weight, easy to cut, and there are a tremendous number of compatible fittings and valves available. Copper pipe is joined by soldering, and the techniques are quite simple to master (Fig. 8-2).

Copper pipe is a relatively soft material, making it prone to denting and deformation if not handled correctly. The best way to cut copper pipe is with a tubing cutter. This cutter exerts an even pressure on the pipe and always cuts a square end. A fine-toothed hacksaw can also be used, but great care must be taken not to put too much downward pressure on the pipe, causing it to flatten out of round.

To use a tubing cutter, rotate the handle to open up the jaws wide enough to slip the cutter over the pipe, then tighten it down again until the cutting wheel is in light contact with the pipe. Rotate the cutter one full turn, then tighten the handle slightly. Continue to rotate the cutter, tightening the handle with each rotation, until the pipe has been cut through. Use a pipe reamer or a round file to smooth the cut and remove any burrs.

After the pipe has been cut, test fit it for length using the proper fittings. When you're certain the layout is correct, disassemble the joints and prepare them for soldering.

The key to successful soldering is a clean joint. Using emery cloth or one of the small wire brushes made specifically for use with copper pipe, clean the end of the pipe until it is bright and shiny. Be sure you clean an area that is at least equal to the depth

the pipe will penetrate into the fitting, and clean all around the pipe. Next, clean the inside of the fitting. The importance of this cleaning step cannot be overemphasized, as dirt or corrosion on the pipe is the most common reason for joint failure.

After the pipe and fitting have been cleaned, use a small brush and apply a liberal amount of paste flux to the end of the pipe. Insert the pipe into the fitting, and adjust everything so that it's properly aligned before soldering the joint.

Using a propane torch, apply heat to the joint until the fitting begins to change color. Remove the torch, and touch the tip of a piece of wire solder to the joint. If the joint has been properly cleaned and heated, the solder will instantly be drawn up into and around the joint, forming a seal as it dries. If the solder will not draw up, apply more heat and try again. (Valves and large fittings will require more heating time than small fittings will.) Do not use the flame from the torch to melt the solder. If, after reheating, the joint still will not take solder, let it cool, then disassemble it and clean and flux it again.

Because the heat may weaken existing joints, it is best to solder all the joints on a particular fitting at the same time. For example, if you are installing a T fitting, you should have all three pipes in place, and then solder the three joints simultaneously. If this is not possible and you need to work right next to an existing joint, wrap the joint with a wet towel to keep it cool.

Soldered joints can also be disassembled if necessary. Simply heat the joint until the solder becomes liquid, then gently tap the joint apart with a hammer. Completely clean and flux any pipe and fittings you intend to reuse.

Galvanized Pipe

For years, threaded galvanized metal pipe and fittings were standard for almost all plumbing installations. This type of pipe, however, is prone to interior corrosion after years of use, in some cases reducing the interior diameter of the pipe to little more than a pinhole.

Working with galvanized metal pipe takes considerably more effort than using copper. Cuts can be made with a hacksaw, but a larger, heavier ver-

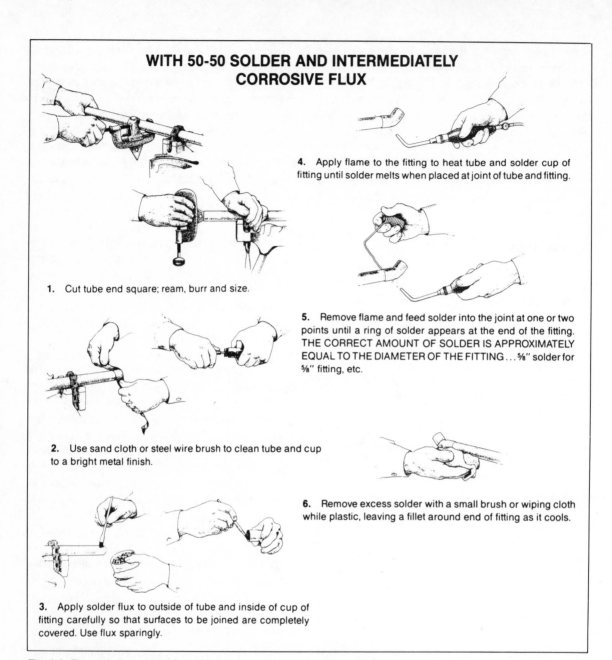

WITH 50-50 SOLDER AND INTERMEDIATELY CORROSIVE FLUX

1. Cut tube end square; ream, burr and size.

2. Use sand cloth or steel wire brush to clean tube and cup to a bright metal finish.

3. Apply solder flux to outside of tube and inside of cup of fitting carefully so that surfaces to be joined are completely covered. Use flux sparingly.

4. Apply flame to the fitting to heat tube and solder cup of fitting until solder melts when placed at joint of tube and fitting.

5. Remove flame and feed solder into the joint at one or two points until a ring of solder appears at the end of the fitting. THE CORRECT AMOUNT OF SOLDER IS APPROXIMATELY EQUAL TO THE DIAMETER OF THE FITTING...⅝" solder for ⅝" fitting, etc.

6. Remove excess solder with a small brush or wiping cloth while plastic, leaving a fillet around end of fitting as it cools.

Fig. 8-2. The techniques used for soldering copper pipe and fittings (Courtesy of Nibco, Inc.).

sion of the tubing cutter is usually used. After cutting, the pipe must be threaded, using either a ratcheting hand threader or a power threader. Both the cutter and the pipe threader can be rented if you have a need for them.

After the pipe has been threaded, it is assembled using compatible threaded fittings. A paste type of pipe joint compound should be used on the joints to ensure a leakproof seal, or joint tape can be wrapped around the threads.

If you have a fair amount of plumbing to do, you'll usually find it easier to transition from the existing galvanized plumbing to one of the other materials.

Plastic Water Pipe

A way to further simplify the running of hot and cold water lines is through the use of plastic pipe. Cholorinated polyvinyl chloride (CPVC) is a rigid pipe that is suitable for both hot and cold water applications. Like ABS or PVC, it is joined with a liquid solvent adhesive, and is quite easy to work with.

Polybutylene pipe (PB) is a flexible plastic tubing that can also be used for both hot and cold water lines. It is sold in rolls, and has the very distinct advantage of being flexible enough to make a number of jogs and turns without fittings. PB pipe is used quite extensively in the manufacture of mobile homes, but is still not seen that often in residential construction. Assembly is made using compression nuts and fittings, adhesive, or crimp connectors, depending on the type of pipe and the fittings used.

The main disadvantage to plastic pipe for water lines are the plastic valves, which in most cases are not of the quality and durability seen in metal valves. Check these components carefully when purchasing plastic pipe. You'll also need to check with the building department to make sure the pipe you've chosen is approved for residential use.

TRANSITIONS BETWEEN MATERIALS

A definite advantage to many of today's plumbing materials is the ease with which they can be adapted to whatever materials your home is currently plumbed with. Transition fittings are made specifically for virtually every combination of materials you're likely to run into, giving you a considerable amount of flexability with your choices.

DWV Transitions

Cast iron pipe was used extensively in residential construction for many years, and as a result, probably the most common transition situation

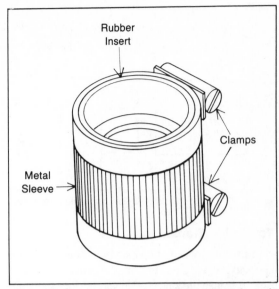

Fig. 8-3. A band clamp for joining cast iron pipe, or for making transitions between pipes of different materials.

you're likely to encounter is adapting ABS (or PVC) pipe to existing cast iron. The transition is simple with the use of a device called a band clamp (Fig. 8-3).

A *band clamp* is simply a thick rubber sleeve with a flexible metal band around the outside, to which two worm drive clamps are attached. To use the clamp, first slide the metal band onto the cast iron pipe. Next, the rubber sleeve is slipped over the end of the cast iron pipe until it bottoms out against the stop, inside the sleeve. Insert the ABS pipe into the sleeve until it, too, bottoms out, then slide the band over the outside of the sleeve. Tighten the two clamps securely with a screwdriver or nut driver, and you'll have a secure, leakproof joint that can be easily disassembled should the need arise.

Band clamps in various sizes can also be used to adapt ABS pipe to large diameter galvanized pipe, which was often used in conjunction with cast iron pipe for running vent lines. For transitions between ABS and other types of sewer lines, such as clay, a similar device called a Caulder coupling is used. In each case, select the appropriate clamp for the transition you're making, and install it as outlined previously.

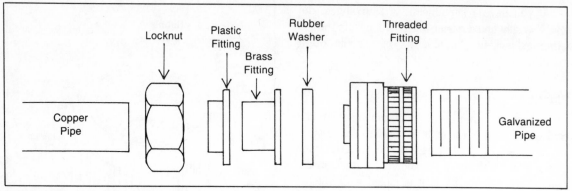

Fig. 8-4. The components of a dielectric union, used for joining copper pipe to galvanized.

Water Line Transitions

For the common transition between galvanized pipe and copper pipe, two methods are commonly used. Because the zinc used in galvanizing pipe combines with copper in a corrosive reaction if joined directly, the two materials must be separated by a third material. One method is to attach a treaded coupling to the end of both the galvanized pipe and the copper pipe, and join the two with a threaded brass nipple, thereby keeping the two pipes separated.

A more common method is the use of a dielectric union (Fig. 8-4). This specialized union has one threaded end for attaching to the galvanized pipe, a slip fitting end for soldering to the copper pipe, and a lock nut which joins the two halves together. Rubber and fiber washers isolate the two halves to prevent direct contact. Dielectric unions are simple to install, and offer the added advantage of a union fitting should disassembly of the joint become necessary.

For transitions between galvanized and any of the various plastic pipes, slip to thread fittings are available. Chemical reactions are not a problem, so the connection is simplified. Simply glue the slip portion of the fitting to the plastic pipe, then thread the galvanized pipe into it.

ROUGH PLUMBING

The sink is the single most critical element of the rough plumbing procedure. If possible, the sink location should be left unchanged to simplify the plumbing. If cabinet changes necessitate moving the sink's location, you'll need to move the waste line, the vent line, and the water lines. Move the waste and vent lines first, as these are larger and require more space. The water lines can be worked in around them.

If the house was not plumbed with plastic pipe originally, use one of the transition methods detailed above and adapt to ABS. Extend a 2 inch line to the location of the new sink, maintaining the necessary fall, then install an elbow and bring the line up through the floor into the wall or cabinet. Install a $1\frac{1}{2}$-×-$1\frac{1}{2}$-×-2-inch sanitary tee fitting (Fig. 8-5), on the end of the 2 inch line. If the sink is at the end of the run off soil line, install a cleanout fitting with a cap on the end of the line. Your plumbing supplier can help you out with the proper fittings.

The upper $1\frac{1}{2}$-inch outlet on the sanitary tee extends up to the vent, which needs to either tie back into the original vent line or extend up through the roof by itself. The center $1\frac{1}{2}$-inch outlet will receive the line from the trap.

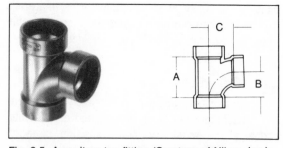

Fig. 8-5. A sanitary tee fitting (Courtesy of Nibco, Inc.).

Tie onto the ends of the existing water lines with the same material as what's there (Fig. 8-6), or transition to copper or plastic as described above if desired. Route the lines to the new sink location and bring them up into the wall or cabinet. Point the lines into the cabinet and cap them temporarily until the stop valves can be installed (Fig. 8-7).

Loop Vents

If the new sink will be installed in an island or a peninsula where venting up through the roof is impossible, you can use a loop vent instead. In place of the elbow where the waste line comes up from below the floor, install a tee (Fig. 8-8). Extend out from the tee horizontally about a foot and install an elbow, pointing up (Fig. 8-8). From the elbow and the top of the tee, extend pipes up about three feet, inside the peninsula or island cabinet. Top the pipes with elbows, and complete the installation with a length of pipe between the elbows, forming a loop. The air trapped in the loop maintains the necessary atmospheric pressure to keep the waste system operating.

TOPPING OUT

Connecting the appliances and fixtures to the rough plumbing is referred to as *topping out*. The procedures and materials have become standardized and simplified to the point where almost anyone can handle them with basic tools and a little patience. The basics for most common installations are outlined below, but be sure and refer to the specific manufacturer's instructions that accompany each unit.

Sinks and Faucets

You'll find it easiest to attach the faucet (Fig. 8-9), to the sink before the sink is installed. This greatly simplifies access to the nuts that hold the faucet in place. Begin by placing the gasket under the faucet, then set the faucet in place on the sink, feeding the connection tubes down through the appropriate holes. Install the under-sink washers as detailed in the manufacturer's instructions, then install the nuts. Center the faucet on the sink, and tighten the nuts.

The basket strainer is another item that you'll find easier to install first. Begin this installation by

Fig. 8-6. Installing a tee fitting into an existing run to extend a water line to the new sink location.

Fig. 8-7. The water and waste lines are extended up into the sink cabinet. The water lines have been capped and the waste line (top center) has been temporarily plugged. Note the cleanout fitting and plug (center).

Fig. 8-8. The tee and elbow fittings that make up the lower part of the loop vent.

placing a bead of plumber's putty under the rim of the basket strainer flange (Fig. 8-10), then insert the strainer body into the sink hole and press the flange down into contact with the sink. From underneath, install the rubber gasket, the metal washer, and then the metal lock nut. Using a pipe wrench or large adjustable pliers, tighten the nut securely, then clean up any excess putty that is squeezed out from under the flange.

The sink portion of the garbage disposal is installed in the same manner. Place a bead of plumber's putty under the flange; press the fitting into the sink hole, then install the appropriate washers and other fittings from underneath, following the manufacturer's instructions. The garbage disposal itself will be installed later.

The procedure for installing the sink will vary with the type of sink and the kind of countertop you're using. The four basic types are:

☐ Separate rim: These are usually enameled steel sinks, and they are held in place through the use of a separate, stainless steel sink rim and a set of special screw clamps. The clamps hook into the rim, and when screwed down, they exert pressure against both the sink and the countertop.

☐ Self-rimming: These sinks have a finished, rounded-over lip that does not require any other type of rim. They are usually installed on top of the counter and held in place with a bead of adhesive caulking under the rim.

☐ Stainless steel: Stainless steel sinks are similar to both the separate rim and the self-rimming sinks. They have a finished, rounded-over edge, and also have a channel welded in place under the rim. Special clamps hook into this channel and are screwed down to hold the sink in place against the countertop.

☐ Tiled-in: Any of the above types of sinks can also be tiled into place. The sink is simply set on the tile decking, then the rim is tiled over, holding the sink in place and giving it a recessed appearance. In the case of the enameled steel sink nor-

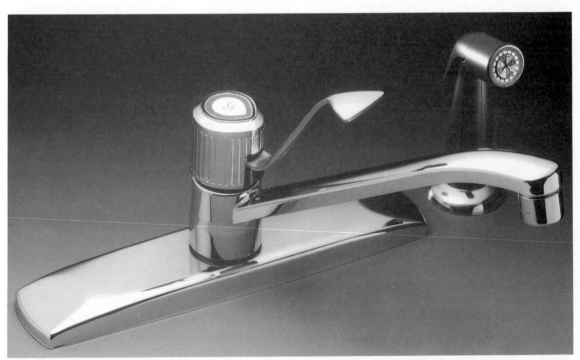

Fig. 8-9. A modern single handle kitchen faucet with separate sprayer. This unit would require a four-hole sink (Courtesy of Moen Faucets).

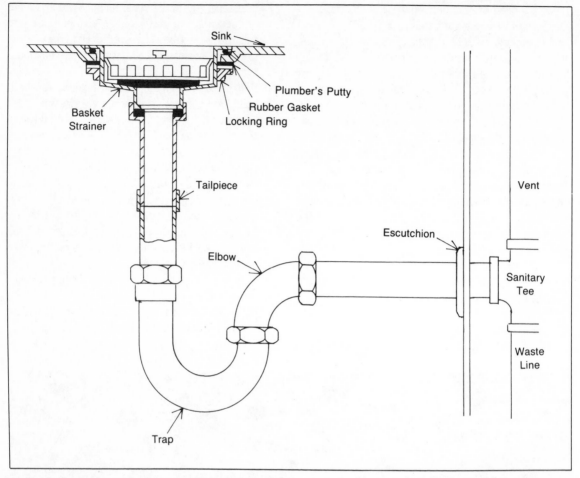

Fig. 8-10. The components of a typical kitchen sink installation, including the basket strainer, tailpiece, and trap.

Waste and Water Lines

The first top out step for the water lines is to install the stop valves. The stop valves are attached to the water lines where they come out of the wall or floor, and are used to start and stop the flow of water to the faucet. These stop valves eliminate the need to shut off the entire house's water supply should work on just the sink be necessary. There are two basic types of stop valves:

☐ Angle stops (Fig. 8-11), in which the inlet and outlet are at right angles to each other. Angle

stops are normally used when the water lines come out of the wall.

☐ Straight stops, in which the inlet and outlet are in line with each other. These are normally used when the water lines come up out of the floor.

Stop valves may have more than one outlet, depending on their intended use. Single outlet valves are used when the valve will only supply water to one fixture, such as just the sink. Double outlet valves should be used to supply two fixtures, for example the icemaker and the cold side of the faucet.

If you are using copper water lines, the stop valves will have a compression nut and sleeve. Simply slip the nut onto the end of the pipe, then the

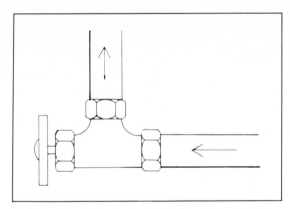

Fig. 8-11. A typical angle stop. Water flow follows the direction of the arrows.

sleeve, then the valve. Tightening the nut will draw the sleeve into the valve and compress it, forming a seal. When you are using plastic pipe, attach a slip to male thread fitting to the end of the pipe, then use a female-threaded valve. Galvanized water lines also use a female-threaded valve.

From the stop valve, you will need a supply line to connect between the valve and the faucet. The easiest lines to use are the new flexible, transparent plastic ones. They have a female threaded cap at each end with a rubber washer, and they make a good, leak-proof seal with a minimum of effort. Their easy flexibility makes aligning the connections simple.

Connecting the waste lines requires a little more effort and patience. Basically, you will need to extend down from the basket strainer with a piece of pipe called a tailpiece. From there, the tailpiece enters a removable trap, then goes out to the soil line in the wall or through the floor. How you accomplish this connection is dependent on the layout of the sinks and where the soil line is.

If you have a two compartment sink, the two basket strainers, or the basket strainer and the garbage disposal, need to be connected to each other before entering the trap. For this, you will need a waste outlet tee fitting, which has all the parts needed to make the connection. If you are entering a soil line that is relatively centered to the sinks, then you will want to use a center outlet tee (Fig. 8-12). If the soil line is near one end or the other, use an end outlet tee (Fig. 8-13).

By using a combination of the proper waste lines and a variety of elbows, you can make the necessary connections without too much difficulty. Work slowly, measuring and aligning the pipes carefully at each step. If necessary, there are flexible tailpieces on the market which can simplify an otherwise stubborn alignment.

Connecting the Dishwasher

There are three basic connections you will need to make to hook up a built-in dishwasher; water, waste and electricity. The water and waste connections will be covered here; the electrical connections will be dealt with in Chapter 9.

You will find it easiest to install the water and waste lines in the cabinet first, before sliding the dishwasher into place. The water line is 3/8- or 1/2-inch copper tubing, depending on the manufacturers recommendations. The waste line is a piece of 3/8-inch rubber hose. Both of these items are sold by the foot, so measure carefully and then buy both several feet longer then you need, to allow for bending and hookups.

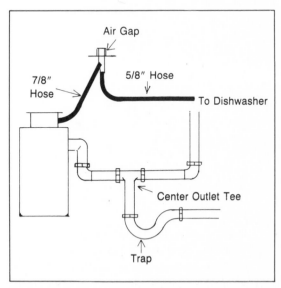

Fig. 8-12. A center outlet tee assembly for connecting the two compartments of a double sink. This installation, which is fairly common, uses an air gap in the drain line between the dishwasher and the garbage disposal.

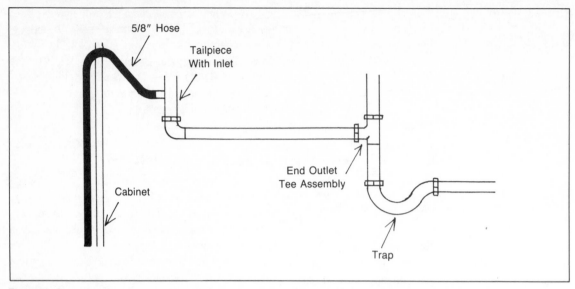

Fig. 8-13. An end outlet tee assembly, used to connect a double compartment sink when the waste line is near the end of the sinks rather than centered. A special tailpiece with an inlet pipe is used in place of a garbage disposal to receive the dishwasher drain line.

You will need to drill two holes through the side of the cabinet between the sink and the dishwasher. They should both be as far to the back of the cabinet as possible; one near the very top of the cabinet, large enough for the waste line, and one near the floor of the cabinet, large enough for the water line.

Slide the lines through the holes so that enough slack is in the sink cabinet to allow for hookups, and lay the excess on the floor of the dishwasher recess. Now slide the dishwasher into place, adjusting the lines so that they remain clear of the dishwasher machinery and extend under the dishwasher all the way to the front of the recess. Adjust the leveling legs on the dishwasher as necessary for a good fit, and secure the unit in place by driving two screws up through the mounting brackets into the underside of the countertop.

☐ Water line connections: You will need to provide a double outlet stop valve on the hot water pipe in order to connect the dishwasher. One outlet goes up to the faucet, the other outlet goes over to the dishwasher. The outlet sizes will need to correspond to the sizes of the two water supply lines.

Route the copper water line from the dishwasher to the valve, and connect it using the compression nut and sleeve provided with the valve. Be very careful when bending the copper line into place—too much pressure or too sharp a bend will crease the tube and restrict or stop the water flow. Route the other end of the line to the water inlet under the dishwasher, and connect it in the same manner.

☐ Waste line connections: On the underside of the dishwasher tub you will find a small pump with a single, plastic outlet. This outlet is the connection point for one end of the $\frac{5}{8}$-inch waste line. Simply slip it over the outlet and clamp it in place with a worm drive clamp.

If you are using a garbage disposal, the other end of the line is attached to the inlet pipe extending out from the neck of the disposal, which is designed for a $\frac{7}{8}$-inch hose. There are two ways of making this connection. If you are using an air gap, which is required by some building departments to prevent siphoning, install the air gap in an unused hole in the sink, or in a hole drilled in the countertop. Route the waste line to the $\frac{5}{8}$-inch side of the air gap (Fig. 8-12), and install it with a worm clamp. Extend a short piece

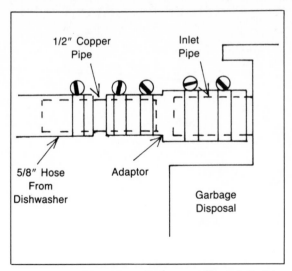

1/2" Copper Pipe

Inlet Pipe

5/8" Hose From Dishwasher

Adaptor

Garbage Disposal

Fig. 8-14. An adaptor fitting used to connect the ⅝-inch dishwasher drain hose to the ⅞-inch pipe on the garbage disposal when an air gap is not used.

of ⅞-inch rubber hose between the air gap and the disposal, clamping both ends in place.

If you are not using an air gap, be sure the drain hose passes through the cabinet wall at a height above the top of the dishwasher tub to prevent siphoning (Fig. 8-13), and route the hose to the disposal. Slip a 6-inch piece of ½-inch cop-per pipe halfway into the hose and clamp it in place. A special ⅝- to ⅞-inch adaptor (Fig. 8-14), available at plumbing stores, is used to make the connection between the other end of the copper pipe and the inlet tube on the garbage disposal.

There is a small knockout inside the garbage disposal that seals the inlet tube in case the disposal is used without a dishwasher. Be sure you remember to knock the plug out with a hammer and screwdriver prior to installation.

If no disposal is used, you will need a special tailpiece for the sink (Fig. 8-13) which has a side inlet tube that receives the waste line. Route the line from the dishwasher to the tailpiece, and make the connections using worm drive clamps.

The final step in any plumbing installation is to carefully check for leaks. Turn the stop valves on one at a time, and systematically check each connection to be sure it's dry. Run water in each compartment of the sink to check the waste lines, then stopper each compartment and fill them with water to check the seal around the basket strainers. Finally, run the dishwasher through a complete cycle and check the waste and water connections. Tighten any loose connections as necessary.

Chapter 9

Electrical Wiring

MOST KITCHENS CONTAIN MORE ELECTRICAL WIRing than any other room in the house. With lighting, stationary appliances, and portable appliance circuits, there's a lot of wiring packed in a fairly small amount of space. A new kitchen usually means more wiring for new appliances and relocated circuits. While the cabinets are out and the walls are open is your chance to update the wiring and make it more convenient.

There are several basic wiring requirements which are common to all kitchen layouts. Your kitchen will probably contain all or most of these, and perhaps more, depending on its size and layout. Using the floor plan and cabinet layouts you developed in earlier chapters, take some time to plot out an electrical plan. A comprehensive plan takes only a short time to draw up, and it ensures that you'll get all the wiring you need in the kitchen while eliminating waste.

If you are having a designer draw up your plans, they should also provide an electrical plan for you or your electrician to work from (Fig. 9-1), or your electrician can draw one out for you if you have any questions. No matter who provides the plan, it's often best to have it checked by an electrical inspector at your local building department. They can tell you if it's properly and safely laid out, and if your plans are in compliance with local electrical codes.

BASIC CIRCUITS

Don't skimp on the placement of receptacles in the kitchen. They make the areas more convenient, and they eliminate having to use extension cords, a real safety hazard. Plan on providing at least one receptacle for any counter space in the kitchen or dining room that is 12 inches or wider (any counter space that is broken up by a cooktop, sink, or refrigerator is considered by the Electrical Code to be a separate counter space). Space the receptacles no more than 6 feet apart on long counter runs, four to 5 feet apart is preferable for greater convenience.

Every kitchen contains certain basic circuits, which provide a safe and convenient layout for the electrical wiring. These circuits include:

☐ Small appliance circuits: Due to the large number of portable appliances that are used, every kitchen must contain at least two 20 amp circuits for the receptacle. These circuits should be divided so that roughly half the kitchen is on each circuit, and can also include outlets in the pan-

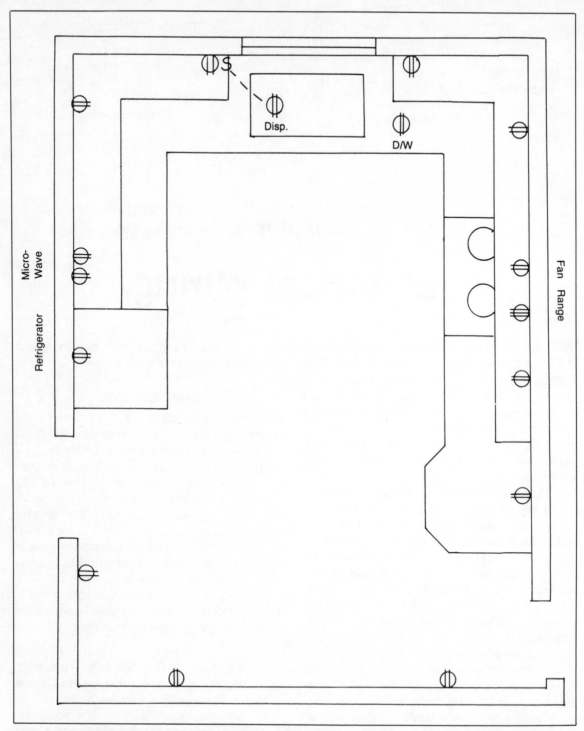

Fig. 9-1. A complete plan for the electrical outlets and appliance connections. The other part of the electrical plan, the lighting and switch layout, is shown in Fig. 6-9.

try, breakfast room, dining room, and living room. These two circuits should be for receptacles only, and should not include any lighting.

☐ Lighting circuit: Provide at least one 15-amp circuit for the lighting, including overhead and undercounter lights.

☐ Microwave circuit: If your kitchen has a built-in microwave oven, it should have its own 15-amp circuit.

☐ Dishwasher/garbage disposal: Provide a separate, 20-amp circuit for the dishwasher and/or the garbage disposal.

☐ Trash compactor: The trash compactor should be on its own circuit, also.

☐ Stationary appliance circuits: Each stationary appliance, such as a cooktop or an oven, requires a separate, dedicated (serving that appliance only) circuit. The circuit size must be sufficient to serve the appliance's amperage rating, as listed on the appliance nameplate.

☐ Laundry room: If your new kitchen will contain a laundry room, you will need to provide a 110-volt, 20-amp circuit for the washer and a 220-volt, 30-amp circuit for the dryer. At least one receptacle other than the one for the washer is also required.

CIRCUIT SIZES

Most residential wiring today is done using non-metallic sheathed cable, known simply as NM cable or by the common trade name "Romex." NM cable contains three or more individual wires, each with their own color-coded insulation, all wrapped by one common outer jacket of insulation for convenience.

The number of the conductors grouped together in the cable is dependent on the type of circuit you're running. For example, most 110-volt circuits require three wires (including the ground wire), while some types, such as those for three-way lights, require a four-wire cable. Likewise, most 220-volt circuits will require a four-wire cable.

Wire size is governed by the amperage of the circuit. You can refer to Table 9-1 to determine the size of the wire you'll need.

Table 9-1. Wire Size As Determined by Circuit Amperage.

Circuit Size	Wire Size
15 amp	14 gauge
20 amp	12 gauge
30 amp	10 gauge
40 amp	8 gauge
50 amp	6 gauge

GROUNDING AND COLOR CODING

To ensure safety and universal wiring practices, all electrical wiring today is color coded. The individual wires in the cable will each have a colored jacket to simplify the proper installation. Hot wires will be colored black, red, or any color other than white, green or bare. The neutral wire is always white, and the ground wire is either bare or color coded green.

All new wiring in your home is required to be grounded, whether the existing wiring is grounded or not. In some instances, building officials will make you upgrade your existing wiring if it is ungrounded and appears unsafe.

Grounding is accomplished through the use of a third wire in the circuit: the bare or green-jacketed one. The ground wire connects all the metal parts within the electrical system to the service panel, and from there to a ground source, usually a cold water pipe, or a rod buried in the earth or in the building's foundation. When connecting appliances, fixtures, receptacles, or any other metal electrical component, always look for the green grounding screw, and be certain the ground wire in the NM cable is connected to it.

BASIC WIRING TECHNIQUES

As mentioned earlier, the bulk of residential wiring is done through the use of type NM cable, which is safe, convenient, and easy to work with. You can safely run NM cable in walls, under the floor, in the basement or crawlspace—anywhere the cable will be protected from abrasion and contact. If you need to run the cable outdoors, it needs to be protected in conduit. If the cable will be buried in the ground, use sunlight and burial protected cable, which is available just about anywhere that regular NM cable is found.

Wiring is normally the last thing done in the kitchen, after the tearout, rough carpentry, and rough plumbing are completed. This allows you to route the cable around obstacles, and gives you access to open areas before the drywall is patched.

New circuits originate at the service panel, and extend from there to the first outlet or fixture in line. Dedicated circuits, those which serve only one appliance or receptacle, must extend directly from the panel to the appliance, with no interruptions. Placing a splice in a junction box on a dedicated circuit gives someone the opportunity to unknowingly tap into the circuit at a later date, creating the possibility of a dangerous overload on the circuit.

Your wiring should be extended between fixtures and boxes in the most direct manner possible, and installed so as to be easily concealed, both for safety and appearance. This is most easily accomplished by boring holes through the centers of the studs and pulling the cable through between boxes. If the studs are not open, as is often the case in remodeling, the next most direct route is usually under the house, in the basement or crawlspace.

To accomplish this, first you need to know which wall cavity you wish the wire to come up in. Then, drill a small hole through the floor, up against the wall (the baseboards or carpeting will cover the hole, or you can fill it to match the surrounding floor) (Fig. 9-2). Go under the house, locate the hole (it's easier if you leave the bit in temporarily), measure in toward the wall about two inches, and drill a hole up. You can then fish the wire up from underneath. If you find it easier to work down from the attic, the same method of drilling and fishing can be used.

Type NM cable, because of its flexibility, needs to be properly supported. Using cable staples, staple the cable within eight inches of any box. It should also be stapled or otherwise supported every 4½ feet. Passing it through drilled holes in studs or joists is sufficient support. Leave approximately 6 inches of free wire at each box for making connections.

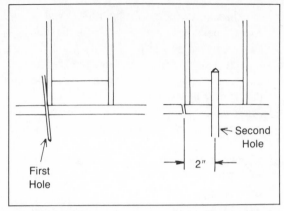

Fig. 9-2. Drilling a small hole through the floor next to the wall can be used to locate the wall from under the house.

ROUGH WIRING LOCATIONS

An important consideration when installing electrical wiring is the *rough-in location*—that particular spot on the wall, floor, or ceiling where a wire is brought in for later hookup. With the number of appliances and lights normally found in the kitchen, rough-in locations need to be carefully figured.

The usual first step is to measure out the actual cabinet dimensions, including fillers and panels, and mark the locations on the walls or the floor. These marks are a tremendous help in visualizing exactly where receptacles, appliances and the other electrical components of the kitchen will be located.

Ceiling-mounted light fixtures are fairly easy to locate. They are usually centered in the room by measuring wall to wall, or are spotted so as to be directly over an island or other specific area. A round fixture box is cut in at the appropriate spot, then the wire is routed to the box for later hookup to the fixture. Fixture boxes (Fig. 9-3), depending on the type, may be mounted by nailing them to a ceiling joist or other wood member, by hanging them from a metal cross bar that is secured between the joists, or by using a special box with flexible metal flanges that spring out behind the drywall and hold the box in place with no other support.

Undercabinet lights need to be laid out with care to be sure the wire does not come out too high, where it would be behind the cabinet, or too low,

C-1. (top) BEFORE, this kitchen featured wood cabinets, a breakfast bar, and a sink behind the bar. (bottom) AFTER, the cabinets were replaced, the bar was removed, and the sink was moved to an island to give the kitchen a more spacious look.

C-2. (top) BEFORE, this outdated, 1950s kitchen suffered from green plastic wall panels, mismatched cabinets, and a serious lack of storage and counter space. The owners also wanted to incorporate a kitchen eating area. (bottom) AFTER, the kitchen is bright, cheery, and spacious. The doorway to the right was closed off to create more space, and the new island provides additional counter and eating space. The cooktop is down-venting and needs no hood. The ingenious, custom-built ceiling fixture combines generous fluorescent lighting with built-in tracks, which accommodate steel hooks for hanging pots. (Courtesy of Western Wood Products Association)

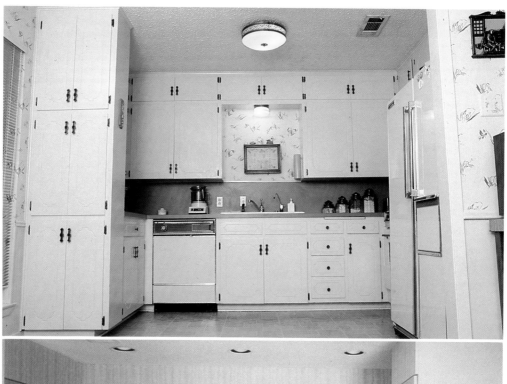

C-3. (top) BEFORE, this compact kitchen had a closed-in feeling, and lacked convenient storage and up-to-date appliances. (bottom) AFTER, the kitchen provides a feeling of greater spaciousness in the same amount of floor area. A wallpapered soffit lowered the cabinets, and the glass-fronted wall units give an open feeling. Lighting was improved, a trash compactor was added, and the inconvenient storage cabinet on the right was converted to hold an oven/microwave combination. The wasted space above the sink was converted to open shelves, and two appliances garages (behind the tambour doors) provide out-of-the-way appliance storage. (Courtesy of Wilsonart)

C-4. (top) The eating area of this kitchen used up vital floor space and gave the room a slightly cluttered feeling. (bottom) The solution was to remove the table and construct a portable island to match the existing cabinets. The island offers extra counter space for preparing meals. (Courtesy of American Olean Tile)

C-5. (left) A fresh coat of paint and a new tile floor complete the makeover. (right) When it's time to eat, the island rolls against the wall to become a table. (Courtesy of American Olean Tile)

C-6. (top) This all-white kitchen sparkles with splashes of red and black accent colors. The spacious island provides extra working and storage space, and breaks up the distance between the refrigerator and the sink. (bottom) There is also space above the cabinets for extra storage or collectibles. Two cooks can fit in this kitchen easily. (Courtesy of Wilsonart)

C-7. (right) In this kitchen, plaster was stripped off the ceiling to expose beams, which were cleaned and stained a dark color. New cabinets were installed and topped off by gold-tone ceramic tile.

(below right) The Spanish motif was carried through to a new archway, which connects the kitchen to the adjacent family room. The upper cabinets were recessed into the wall; tiled-in niches on either side of the arch and an exposed pot rack above it combine to provide the maximum amount of storage space. (Courtesy of American Olean Tile)

C-8. (left) Garden windows are easy to install and can really brighten up a kitchen. They allow a tremendous amount of light in and give extra space for fresh herbs and other greenery. They are available in a variety of sizes to replace a number of standard windows.

(below left) Freestanding, all-in-one appliances like this one can free up a lot of space in a small kitchen. This unit combines a conventional oven, a cooktop, a microwave, and an exhaust hood in just six square feet of floor area.

(below right) When space is at a premium, make the space work for you. Here, cabinets were extended off the kitchen into the adjacent eating area, making room for additional, glass-fronted storage, a quaint, wrought-iron table and chair set, and a washer and dryer. The overhead fan provides light, circulation, and a touch of elegance, and the well-coordinated colors make the room come alive. (Courtesy of Wilsonart)

C-9. (right) Storage abounds in this kitchen, which is typical of some of the features incorporated in today's popular European-look cabinet styles. The bifold corner door and revolving shelves give access to every inch of the corner wall cabinet.

(below right) A pull-out basket adds convenient storage for smaller items, while the molded drawer inserts really organize kitchen drawer clutter.

(below left) The revolving pull-out shelves in the lazy susan provide access to the bottom corner cabinet. (Courtesy of Wilsonart)

C-10. (above) Versatile plastic laminates provide color and form, and show how the unusual can easily be made a part of your next kitchen. This counter shows color sandwiching, here accomplished with Wilsonart Solicor laminate.

(right) Here is a beautiful example of how natural wood can combine with plastic laminate counters and cabinet facings for a stylish, easy-care kitchen.

(below) With the vast array of portable appliances found in the normal kitchen, appliance garages are a popular feature. The tambour top, coordinated to the color of the counters, drops down to keep the normal countertop appliance clutter out of sight. Receptacles concealed in the back of the garages end cord tangles, also. (Courtesy of Wilsonart)

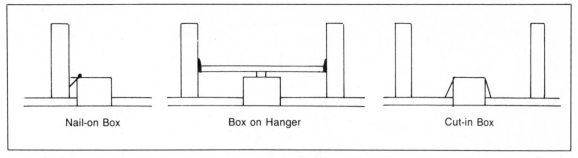

Fig. 9-3. Typical fixture boxes.

where it would be exposed below the light fixture. The normal rough-in height off the floor is 54 inches, which would put the wire right at the bottom of a 30-inch upper cabinet (based on the upper cabinets being 84 inches off the floor at the top). For an 18-inch upper cabinet, the rough-in would be 66 inches up; 69 inches up for a 15-inch cabinet, and 72 inches up for a 12-inch cabinet. These heights are only averages; verify them by marking the actual cabinet heights on the wall and then use them as a guide.

The wire for the undercabinet light should come out near one end or the other of where the fixture will be (Fig. 9-4). For example, if you have a 24-inch-wide cabinet and you are using an 18-inch-long fixture, centering the fixture under the cabinet would leave 3 inches on each side. The wire, therefore, should come out of the wall at the appropriate height and approximately 3 inches in from either edge of the cabinet.

Receptacles that will be above the counters should be centered about 45 inches up off the floor (Fig. 9-5) if the lower cabinets are 36 inches high (with counters), and upper cabinets start 18 inches above the counters. In this way, the receptacles will be centered between the counters and the upper cabinets. If you will be having a single tile backsplash, place the receptacle above the tile. If you will be having a full tile backsplash, try and center the boxes between where the grout lines will be (Fig. 9-6).

If the upper cabinet has a low hanging valence to cover the undercabinet lights, then you may want to move the receptacles down for best appearance. Switches for the undercabinet lights are placed at the same level as the receptacles, and are usually put in double boxes with the receptacle.

Rough-in locations for the appliances need to be a little more exact, and your best bet is to refer to the manufacturer's instructions for their recommendations. For an oven or a cooktop, the wires are usually brought into a box located within the lower cabinet (Fig. 9-7). The appliance itself usually has its wires encased in a length of flexible metal conduit, allowing you sufficient length to make the wiring connections in the cabinet box. The instructions will give you a range of areas within the cabinet (Fig. 9-8), any of which will work with the given length of conduit.

Freestanding ranges are wired using a cord, which comes attached to the appliance. You will need to provide a range outlet box, usually on the wall with the space where the range will sit, just above floor level. After the range is placed in position, it is simply plugged into the receptacle. A range outlet has a different face configuration than a dryer outlet does because of the different amperages, so be certain you are selecting the correct receptacle.

Portable microwave ovens, even when they're being built in, have a standard 110 volt cord and plug on them. You should plan on providing a receptacle within the area of the microwave cabinet where the oven will actually sit (Fig. 9-9), or in the cabinet directly above it. The instructions that come with the microwave installation kit will give you the exact location. If the microwave is part of a conventional oven/microwave oven combination, making the junction box connection in the cabinet will activate both units.

Fig. 9-4. The rough-in location for the wire that will connect to an undercabinet light.

Fig. 9-5. A cut-in box used in an appliance garage to provide an outlet.

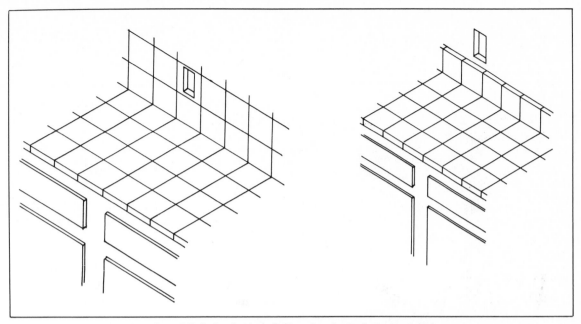

Fig. 9-6. Receptacle locations for a full-tile backsplash (left) and a single-tile backsplash.

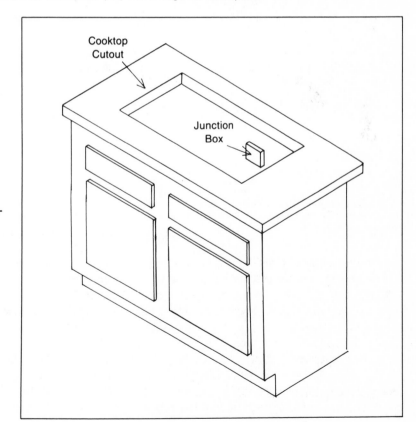

Fig. 9-7. Typical base cabinet junction box location for a cooktop.

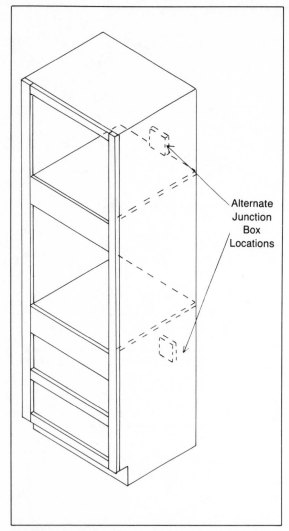

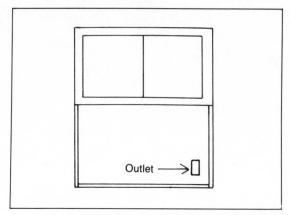

Fig. 9-9. The typical location for a receptacle within a micro-wave cabinet.

Fig. 9-8. Possible junction box locations for a built-in oven. Always refer to the manufacturer's instruction for information on exact locations.

For the dishwasher, just bring a line up into the cavity where the unit will set, and leave about three to four feet of slack. Dishwashers are connected at a junction box located at the lower front of the unit, so you need enough play in the wire to route it to the box and make the connection. The same is true for trash compactors.

Garbage disposals can be either hard wired (connected directly) or plugged in, depending on the brand. In either case, route your wire to a box lo-cated within the sink cabinet. For a hard-wired unit, run a length of conduit out from the box to the dis-posal. If the unit plugs in, simply install a receptacle in the box.

REMOVING WIRING

Kitchen remodeling frequently requires eliminating wiring, also. Care must be taken to move and cap off unneeded circuits safely, preventing dangers from open circuits and eliminating unnecessary load on the service panel.

You can splice 110-volt circuits as necessary to eliminate wires. For example, if you encounter a wire running across an area in the wall that you need to open up (Fig. 9-10), the wire can be traced back to the box it originated from. From that box, a wire can be spliced in and routed around the opening to connect to the next box in line. If you can't trace the line all the way back to its box, cut it and extend it up into the attic and place it into a junction box. Do the same with the other end of the line, then run a new wire between the two junction boxes. The same is true if you need to eliminate a receptacle, or move it to a new location.

For 220-volt circuits, the line needs to be elimi-nated at the service panel and, if possible, the wir-ing removed and discarded. This prevents anyone from tapping into the wires incorrectly in the future. When using either 110-volt or 220-volt wires, the circuit should never be capped off and left in the wall.

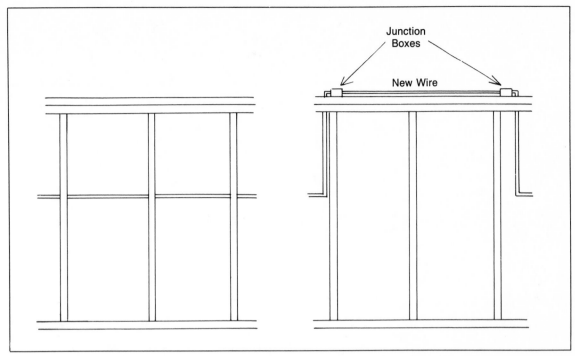

Fig. 9-10. Use junction boxes to relocate an electrical cable around an area of a wall that will be opened up.

It must always be disconnected and enclosed in a junction box with a blank cover.

If you have questions about running new wires or eliminating wiring, talk with an electrician or an electrical inspector. It's essential that all the wiring you do be correct for the sake of your safety, so if you have any doubts, resolve them before proceeding.

Chapter 10

Finishing the Odds and Ends

KITCHEN REMODELING OFTEN REQUIRES BITS AND pieces of many skills and trades. Rough carpentry, finish carpentry, sheet metal work, door and window hanging, drywall; all of these, and more, can be involved to some extent in just about any kitchen. It's one of the things that makes remodeling a kitchen fun and challenging.

This chapter will look at some of the tools, materials, and skills you may find yourself needing on your kitchen project. Work in some of the areas covered is done before the cabinets are installed, and some is done after. They've been grouped together here for your convenience in learning about them. As with wiring and plumbing, you'll need to select those aspects of the work you're comfortable with, and consider hiring out the others.

ROUGH CARPENTRY

There are many areas where rough carpentry skills will be needed on a kitchen remodel; framing new walls and openings, constructing soffits, installing blocking, removing existing walls, and more. These tasks will require basic carpentry tools and abilities. Even removing a bearing wall is well within the range of the average do-it-yourselfer.

Framing Walls

When constructing a new wall, the basic wall unit consists of a top and bottom horizontal plate and vertical studs. When a house is being constructed, these wall components are assembled lying flat and then are tilted up into position. With remodeling, it's often not possible to construct the wall in this manner; instead, it is constructed in place.

Construction begins by laying out the plates. The standard material for constructing interior walls is the 2 × 4 (actual size 1½ × 3½ inches, an important fact to bear in mind as you proceed), so select two straight 2 × 4s and cut them to the proper length for the wall you're building. Begin at the left end of one board (Fig. 10-1), measure in 1½ inches, mark a line, then draw an X to the left of the line. This indicates the location of the first stud.

For stud spacing of 16 inches on center, measure from the end of the board and draw a line at 15¼ inches. Mark an X to the right of the line. This indicates that the stud should be placed against the line and on the right side of it. Because the stud is 1½ inches wide, placing the edge at 15¼ inches will place the center at 16. From this second stud mark, mark the rest of the board in 16-inch increments,

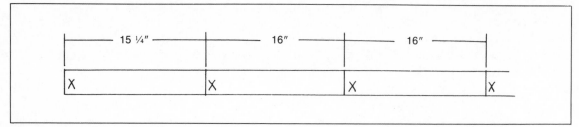

Fig. 10-1. Plate layout for studs on 16-inch centers.

placing an X on the right side of the line, until you reach the end.

The first board is the bottom plate for your wall. Place the second board next to it, align the ends, and transfer the lines and the X's to the second board. This is the top plate.

Measure the distance from the floor to the ceiling, subtract three inches (the thickness of the two plates) and cut your studs to this length. You may have noticed that your wall has only one top plate, while the existing walls in the house have two. Doubled top plates are standard in residential construction, with the second plate overlapping the first to tie the walls together. In remodeling, the second plate is often omitted on non-bearing walls. If you choose to double the top plate, remember to subtract 4½ inches from the floor to ceiling measurement when cutting your studs.

If the wall is to be assembled flat and then raised into position, lay the studs out on edge and nail the plates to them. With the assistance of a helper, raise the wall into place, check it for plumb, then nail it to the floor and the cross walls or other supports.

When remodeling, space often will not permit a new wall to be assembled and raised (Fig. 10-2). Instead, begin by nailing the bottom plate into place on the floor. Place the first stud in place against a cross wall, plumb it carefully to be sure the wall will not be leaning in or out, then nail it to the cross wall. Repeat this for the stud at the other end. Next, take the top plate and slip it between the ceiling and the tops of the two end studs. Finally, put the remaining studs in place; align them to your marks, top and bottom, then toenail them to the top and bottom plates with 10d or 12d nails.

Fig. 10-2. A wall that has been built in place to close off a doorway.

Framing Openings

Wall openings (Fig. 10-3), consist of a header, which carries the load over the opening; trimmers, which support the header; and a rough sill, which forms the bottom of the opening. The size of the header depends on the width of the opening. As a

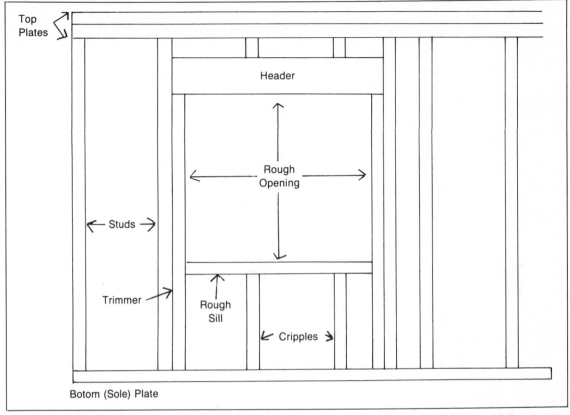

Fig. 10-3. The components of a framed opening in a wall. The rough opening needs to be sized accurately for whatever will be placed in the opening.

rule of thumb, a 4 × 4 will span up to 4 feet, a 4 × 6 up to 6 feet, etc. You'll want to verify this with the building department by checking their span tables.

The actual size of the opening you frame is known as the rough opening. The rough opening needs to conform to the size of the window, door, or whatever will be placed in the opening. Rough opening sizes can be obtained from the manufacturer of whatever window or door you'll be using.

For openings in the ceiling (Fig. 10-4), such as for a skylight, you need to box between the joists to create a rough opening of the proper size. If the joists need to be cut, headers of the same size material as the joists are placed across the ends of the opening to carry the cut joists. The headers and trimmers should be doubled for large openings.

REMOVING A WALL

Another common situation encountered in kitchen remodeling is the need to remove a wall. Existing walls can be non-bearing (also called curtain or partition walls) meaning they don't support anything except themselves, or they can be bearing, meaning they support an additional load. This load may be ceiling joists, second floor joists, rafters, or other structural members. Unless you can determine for certain that a wall is non-bearing, treat it as a bearing wall.

The first step in removing the wall is to take the weight off it (Fig. 10-5). This is done by constructing a temporary wall on either side of it, supporting the ceiling. This temporary wall is merely a matter of placing a 2-×-4 plate on the floor, then using studs to wedge a second plate up against the

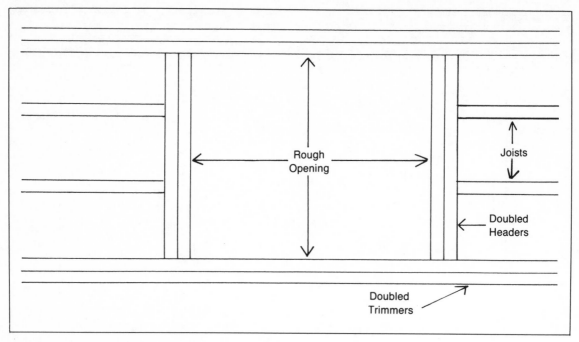

Fig. 10-4. A framed opening in a ceiling or floor.

ceiling. The studs should be cut about ⅛ inch longer than the distance between the plates, so that there is a slight upward pressure on the ceiling when the studs are in place. Toenail the studs in on 24-inch centers.

Cut the ceiling drywall or plaster back on each side of the wall for a distance of about 18 inches. Mark the ceiling with a chalk line and make a clean, straight cut with a reciprocating saw or a hand drywall saw. Taking the time to make a clean cut will simplify patching the drywall later. Strip the drywall off both sides of the wall, also.

With the wall stripped and the load supported on the temporary walls, remove the studs and the bottom plate, leaving the top plate in place. Using this plate as a guide, cut the joists or other members that are resting on top of the wall. Cut just outside the plate on both sides, then remove the plate and the cut sections. The result will be a gap between the joists just over 3½ inches in width.

The final step is to insert a beam into the gap. The beam should be of 4 × material (3½ inches wide) and of a depth in inches equal to the length of the wall in feet. For example, if the wall you're removing is 8 feet long, use a 4 × 8 beam; if it's 10 feet long, use a 4 × 10. For walls over 12 feet in length, consult with the building department for their recommendations.

Slip the beam between the cut joists and rest it on the plates of the cross walls at either end of the wall you've removed. Using appropriate sized joist hangers, connect the cut joists to the new beam. Finally, remove the temporary walls one stud at a time, checking that the weight is being transferred over smoothly to the new beam. The result will be a clean removal, with just one rectangle of drywall to patch in the ceiling.

If you intend to have exposed beams in the kitchen you may wish to leave this supporting beam below the ceiling line also, which simplifies its installation. Additional decorative beams can then be tied into it. See the section on exposed beams.

CONSTRUCTING SOFFITS

Soffits are used with some cabinet installations to make up the difference between the top of the cabinets and the ceiling. The use of soffits and their size

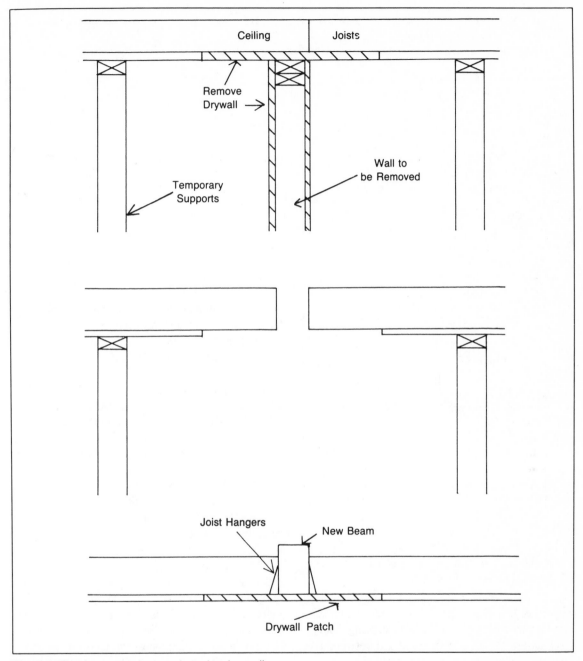

Fig. 10-5. The three steps in removing a bearing wall.

is more a decorating feature than anything else, and should be discussed with your designer prior to the installation of the cabinets. A common alternative to soffits is to finish off the top of the cabinets with a molding or railing, and leave the area above open for display.

Cabinets are installed at a height of 84 inches (7 feet). For a room with an 8-foot ceiling, the soffits

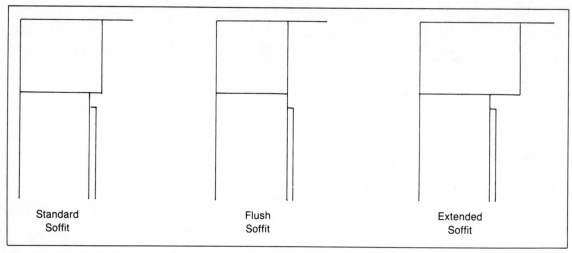

Fig. 10-6. Standard soffit configurations.

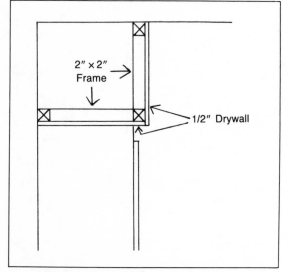

Fig. 10-7. Using 2 × 2s to construct a frame for the soffit, which is then covered with drywall.

the face of the cabinet door. If desired, the over-hang can be greater, or the soffit can be constructed flush with the cabinet faceframe (Fig. 10-6).

The most common method for constructing soffits is to build a two-sided frame out of 2-×-2 lumber (Fig. 10-7). The frame is constructed on the ground before the cabinets are installed. For 12-×-14-inch soffits, nail and toenail the lumber into an 11½-×-13½-inch frame of vertical posts and horizontal stringers. Where there will be tall units or 2-foot-deep uppers, make the soffit 12 × 26 (an 11½-×-25½-inch frame).

Build the soffit in lengths that are comfortable to handle, usually no more than 8 feet. Remember to make the frame long enough so that it will over-hang the ends of the cabinets in an amount equal to how much it overhangs the face.

Mark the ceiling 13½ inches out from the wall with a chalkline, and mark the wall 11½ inches down from the ceiling. Mark the location of the ceiling joists and the wall studs. Using a helper, lift the frame into position and align it with your chalk lines. Nail it in place, making sure the nails hit the studs and joists. Finally, cover the front and the bottom of the frame with ½-inch drywall.

Any easy alternative to the framed soffit is to construct one after the cabinets are installed (Fig. 10-8). For 14-inch soffits, first rip ¾-inch plywood

would be 12 inches high. This measurement can vary, with the important consideration being that ap-proximately 84¼ inches should be left between the floor and the finished bottom of the soffits for easy installation of the cabinets. Any differences will be covered with molding.

The normal depth of the soffit is 14 inches, which allows an overhang of about 1¼ inches past

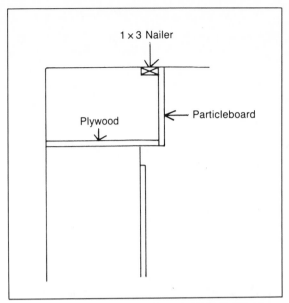

1 × 3 Nailer

Plywood

← Particleboard

Fig. 10-8. An alternate method of constructing a soffit. Place the plywood top on the cabinets first, followed by the nailer, then the front piece of particleboard or drywall.

to 13½ inches (or 25½ inches for tall units and 24-inch-deep uppers). Place the plywood strips on top of the cabinets, flush against the wall and overhanging the front and the ends of the cabinets.

Using a level against the face of the plywood, mark the ceiling at each end of the cabinet run, then snap a chalk line between the marks. This line should be directly over the outer edge of the plywood.

Nail a piece of 1-×-3 lumber to the ceiling, on the inside of the chalk line. Measure from the ceiling to the bottom of the plywood, and rip ½-inch particleboard to this width. Nail the particleboard to the 1 × 3 and plywood to finish off the face of the soffit.

For access to the space taken up by the soffits, you might consider sliding doors instead of a solid face. Simply mount a slotted molding to the top of the cabinets and one to the ceiling, then insert panels of stained plywood in the tracks for doors.

EXPOSED BEAMS

A nice decorative touch in many styles of kitchens is to have exposed beams on the ceiling. If you are removing a wall, one of the beams may be structural, in that it carries the load where the wall was removed. To balance out this beam, additional decorative (nonstructural) beams may be used. Even if there are no structural beams being exposed, you may wish to install false beams for appearance.

Decorative beams take one of three forms. You'll need to make the choice dependent on the particular circumstances and budget of your kitchen:

☐ Solid lumber beams: Beams of solid lumber may be smooth surfaced or rough, depending on the look you want to achieve. Solid beams look authentic and may be necessary to match to exposed structural beams. They are heavy to work with, and must be carefully attached to the ceiling to support the weight. Attachment is usually made by securing blocking over or between the ceiling joists, then bolting down through the blocking into the beams with lag bolts. Because of their size, solid beams may have cracks or checks along the surface—purchase #1 grade lumber to minimize this problem. Solid beams can be painted or stained.

☐ Polyurethane beams: These are beams that are constructed of a formed, high density foam material. The surfaces are textured to resemble heavy, real wood beams, and they are stained to a dark color. They are fairly realistic, very light weight, and easy to install with special clips and hangers.

☐ Fabricated beams (Fig. 10-9): Fabricated beams are made from ¾-inch lumber or plywood, usually in the form of a long, three-sided box. The wood can then be painted or stained and finished to match the cabinets for a very elegant look. Fabricated beams are fairly light, easy to build, and can be constructed in lengths up to about 16 feet without seams (8 feet for plywood). If you construct the beams from plywood, face the exposed edge for best appearance. To install fabricated beams, nail a cleat that's the same width as the inside of the beam to the ceiling joists, slip the beam over the cleat, then nail it in place.

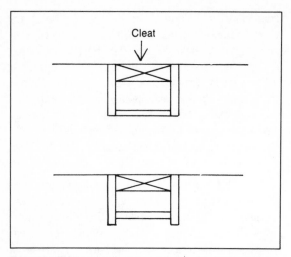

Fig. 10-9. Two methods of constructing fabricated beams for ceiling decoration.

The size and placement of the beams will vary according to taste, but 3 × 5 or 4 × 6 inches is about the right size for a room with 8-foot ceilings. If they are stained, 48-inch spacing between the beams usually looks the best; if they're to be painted, drop the spacing to 24 or 36 inches.

FLOOR UNDERLAYMENT

Another common carpentry task encountered in the kitchen is the need for new floor underlayment. Once the old cabinets have been removed, you may find it necessary to patch in the old underlayment where new cabinets won't cover it. In some cases, it may be wisest to remove all of the old flooring and underlayment and start fresh.

The most common choice for underlayment is ⅜-inch particleboard. It is sold in 4- × -8-foot sheets, and will cover the floor quickly with a minimum number of seams. Use ring shank or screw nails on 6 inch centers, and leave a gap about 1/16 to 1/8 inch between the seams. Lay the sheets in whatever direction gives you the least obvious seams, and stagger the end-to-end seams from sheet to sheet.

Underlayment is usually installed after the cabinets are in. If you install it first, remember that it will raise the height of the cabinets by ⅜ inch, so adjust your soffit and layout heights accordingly.

GARDEN WINDOWS

A popular addition in the kitchen is the garden window. It lets in a lot of light, and its 1-foot depth gives room for potted plants or trays of fresh herbs. They look especially nice if they are installed at counter level and the countertop material is extended into the window.

Garden windows are available in several standard sizes to replace your existing window. If you can't get an exact match, you'll need to open up or close down the existing rough opening to the proper size.

Installing a garden window is a two person job. After the opening has been framed to size, carefully caulk the nailing flange around the window. Lift the window into place from the outside, and have your helper brace it while you go back inside and check the alignment. Nail through the flange into the framing around the window, and finish off the installation with trim to conceal the flange.

To approximate the look and feel of a garden window at less cost, you might consider creating a wider counter area in front of a standard window. This can be done by boxing the window out away from the wall using 2-×-4 or 2-×-6 material (Fig. 10-10), or wider, or can be done by bringing the base cabinets in from the window to create depth (Fig. 10-11). If you opt to bring the base cabinets in, provide framing to support the back side of the counters, and also bring the upper cabinets forward to eliminate a long reach.

SKYLIGHTS

Skylights are a terrific way of bringing a lot of natural light into the kitchen, especially if window area is limited. They can really brighten up the area, and can make even the gloomiest of rooms light and cheery.

Skylights come in two basic forms: flat and dome. Flat skylights (Fig. 10-12), are made of nonyellowing tempered glass, are less obtrusive on the roof, and usually are a little more efficient from an energy standpoint. Dome skylights are made of plastic or plastic compounds, and offer the advantage of a greater light-gathering area.

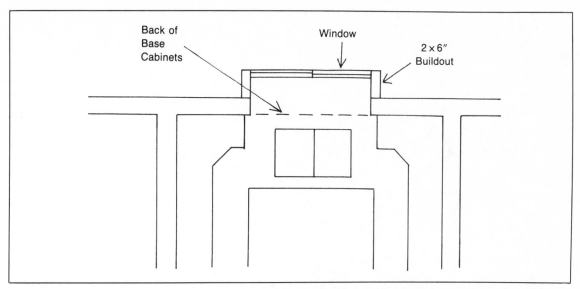

Fig. 10-10. Using 2 × 6 lumber to box out a window, creating a deep counter behind the sink, similar to a garden window.

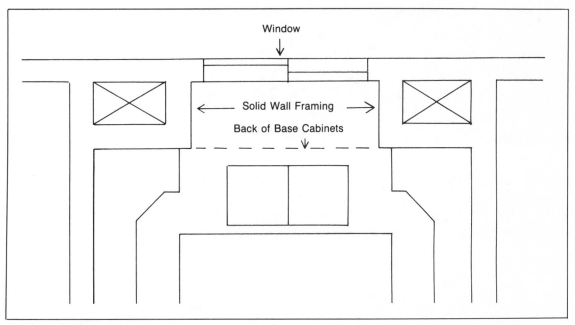

Fig. 10-11. Creating a deep counter in front of a window by bringing the walls in next to the window. This method works especially well with a long room.

If your kitchen has an open ceiling, where the ceiling is the underside of the roof, installation is greatly simplified. You will first need to construct an opening between the joists or beams, following the general guidelines given in the framing section. This will be simplified if you select a skylight size that will fit between the joists without cutting them. Construct a curb according to the manufacturer's

Fig. 10-12. A high-quality flat sky-light (Courtesy of Andersen Windows).

instructions, and mount the skylight. Mounting in-structions vary greatly between manufacturers, so follow the specific instructions for your skylight care-fully. Pay particular attention to the flashing details to ensure a leak-proof installation.

If you have an attic space above the ceiling, you will need to construct a shaft to channel the light from the skylight to the room (Fig. 10-13). Shafts may be straight, angled, or splayed in one or more directions. A straight shaft is the easiest to con-struct. It is the same size as the skylight, and directs

the light straight down. An angled shaft is also the same size as the skylight, but is angled to direct the light to a particular area in the room. Splayed shafts are bigger than the skylight, and are used to get the greatest amount of light possible.

What's usually easiest is to simply open a hole on the ceiling that's the size you want and in the location you'd like it to be. Work up from there, and mount the skylight directly over the opening as much as possible. Use 2 × 4s to connect the corners of the ceiling opening with the corners of the skylight

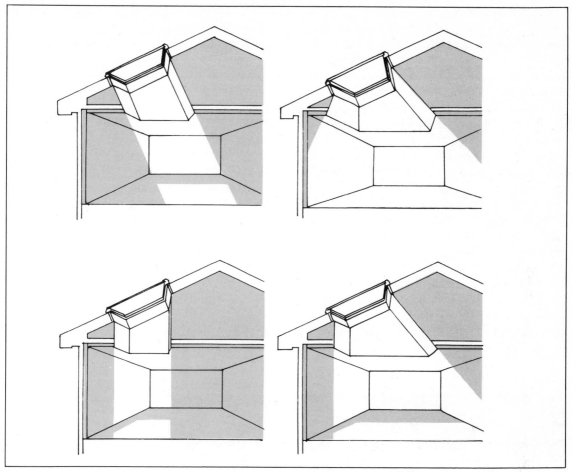

Fig. 10-13. Typical skylight shaft configurations, including straight (top left), angled (bottom left), and splayed (right) (Courtesy of Andersen Windows).

opening, then drywall the inside of the shaft. Painting the shaft flat or semigloss white will increase the amount of reflected light. Don't forget to wrap the outside of the shaft with insulation to minimize heat loss into the attic.

VENTILATION

Proper ventilation is of primary concern in the kitchen. Cooking odors, smoke, and steam all make a good system of venting vital. Ventilation is usually provided at the primary source of odors and steam, the cooktop. This may take the form of a range hood over the cooktop, a downdraft system, or, less often, a ceiling mounted exhaust fan.

Range hoods are probably the most common source of ventilation in the kitchen (Fig. 10-14). They are mounted to a short cabinet directly over the range or cooktop area. Most are vented through the roof or through the wall to the outside. They normally do double duty by providing a light fixture directly over the cooktop. Their depth is sized to fit a 12-inch cabinet, and common widths are 30, 36, and 42 inches. A variety of colors and finishes are available to match the kitchen decor.

Range hoods vary tremendously in their effectiveness. The inexpensive models have a small, bladed fan in them. The fan is mounted horizontally, and the blades resemble those of an airplane propeller. They are only minimally effective, with the smaller models hardly moving any air at all. Better models employ a fan called a squirrel cage, which has one or more sets of horizontal fins that rotate at high speed, moving considerably more air than the blade fans do. Both types have removable grease filters that should be taken out and cleaned regularly.

Range hoods may be ducted or ductless. Ducted hoods vent to the outside through a 6- or 7-inch round pipe, or through a 3½- × -10-inch rectangular pipe. In some instances, you may wish to transition from the rectangular pipe to the round. Special adaptor fittings are available. Use standard sheet metal duct pipe secured with three equally spaced sheet metal screws at each joint. Wrap all the joints with duct tape to seal them. At the roof (Fig. 10-15), terminate the duct in an approved flashing and cap (Fig. 10-16), and seal them carefully against leaks.

Ductless hoods have no duct to the outside. They take in smoke and steam off the cooktop, filter it through one or more filters, then exhaust it back into the room. Ductless hoods are used in some areas where ducting is impossible. They are, however, less effective than ducted hoods, and do nothing to remove steam.

Downdraft systems have a powerful fan mounted between the banks of burners on the cooktop, and exhaust down and to the outside through sheet-metal ducting. Because the fan is placed right at the point of use, these types of systems are very effective while remaining relatively quiet. Follow the same procedures for working with the pipe, and terminate the duct run in a cap approved by the manufacturer.

Whatever type of system you purchase, be certain it has a backdraft damper in it to prevent cold outside air from being brought into the house through the ductwork. Your fan will be most effective if the duct run is kept as short as possible, with a minimum number of elbows.

DRYWALL REPAIRS

With all of the plumbing, electrical wiring, framing, and other work involved in remodeling a kitchen, it's inevitable that some drywall repairs will be required.

Fig. 10-14. A high efficiency ducted range hood. (Courtesy of NuTone).

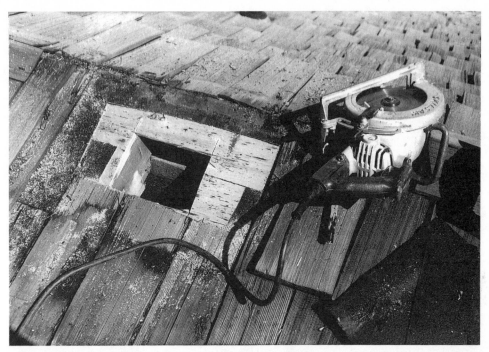

Fig. 10-15. After removing the shingles, use a circular saw to cut through the roof sheathing to create an opening for the vent pipe.

Fig. 10-16. A sheet-metal cap covers the vent pipe. Cut and replace the shingles around the cap, then seal with roof cement to prevent leaks.

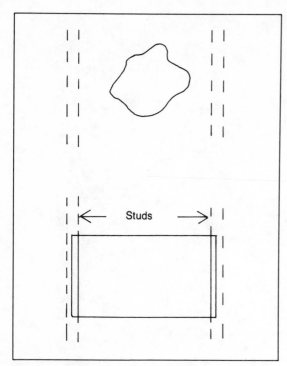

Fig. 10-17. Enlarge any openings in the drywall to the center of the studs to give support for the drywall patch.

Most of these repairs you can easily handle yourself with a little practice.

Drywall is available in two standard thicknesses: ½ inch, and ⅝ inch. You'll be using ½ inch for most standard repairs, but you'll find ⅝-inch drywall handy for patching areas in plastered walls. It's nearly the same thickness as plaster, and saves a lot of work by avoiding wet plastering techniques.

Patching will be simplified if you have made clean cutouts wherever you had to cut into the walls (Fig. 10-17). Cut the existing drywall back to the center of a stud, and square up the edges. Cut a patch to fit the hole neatly, and nail it in with cup-headed drywall nails.

Use joint compound and a 6 inch taping knife to tape the patch. Apply a layer of compound with the knife, then embed the joint tape, centering the tape over the seam. Use the knife to press the tape flat against the drywall without wrinkles, and draw off the excess compound. The layer should be just thick enough to embed and secure the tape at this point.

Allow the compound to dry overnight. If the patch will be concealed by the cabinets, just taping it is enough. If it will be exposed, additional finishing is required. With a 12-inch blade, apply a second layer of compound, feathering it out to both sides of the tape layer. Practice with the blade, applying and scraping off the compound if necessary, until you can apply a smooth coating that is slightly higher over the tape and tapers off to nothing on the surrounding wall.

Allow this second layer to dry, then sand it lightly with 80 or 100 grit paper. If the tape seams are still visible, apply a third coat, tapering it out a full 12 inches to either side of the center of the seam. Let this dry overnight, and sand it as necessary for a smooth, invisible line.

Chapter 11

Installing the Cabinets

BY NOW, YOU'VE REACHED ONE OF THE MOST EX-citing points in the entire project: installing the cabinets. The hours you spend here will bring the kitchen to life, transforming an empty room into the beginnings of reality for your dream kitchen.

As with much of the kitchen remodeling you've done up to this point, you will need only basic carpentry tools for installing the cabinets. You should have available:

☐ A quality 4- to 6-foot level, or a 2-foot level and a long, straight board.

☐ An electric drill and a variety of drill bits, including a countersinking bit.

☐ At least two 4- or 6-inch C-clamps.

☐ A chalk line.

☐ A step ladder.

☐ An accurate tape measure.

☐ A good-quality Phillips screwdriver, medium tip. An electric screw gun, which can be rented or purchased, is a real time saver, or you can get screwdriver tips for your electric drill.

☐ A framing square.

In addition to these and a few other basic tools, you'll need:

☐ A handful of wooden shims or wood shingles.

☐ 1¼-inch and 3-inch flat-head screws. Any good-quality wood screws will work, but your best bet are drywall screws. They are extremely strong, easy to drive and sink, and are a great choice for any woodworking project. (Never use nails for installing cabinets.)

GETTING READY

Before beginning the installation, double check that everything is ready. All of your plumbing and electrical wiring should be complete, all rough carpentry should be out of the way, and all your drywall or plaster patches should be done. Verify by measurement that all your pipes and wires are in the right place, including phone wires.

The kitchen should be completely clean. Remove any debris and unneeded materials, and lay out your tools where they're accessible but not under foot. Finally, give the floor a thorough sweeping.

Refer to your cabinet layout and order sheets and verify that the cabinets you've received are correct. Each carton should have a number on the outside, such as W2430 or B36, that indicates the size of the cabinet. You should be able to check off and verify that you've received everything you ordered.

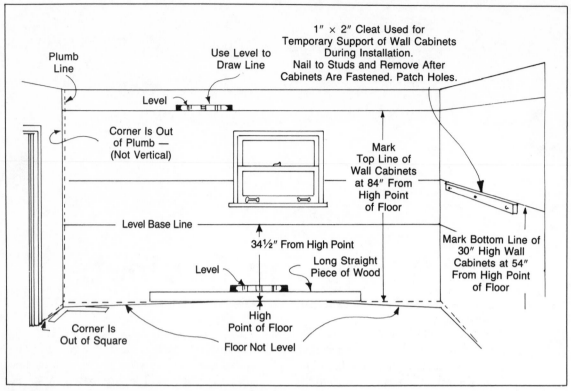

Fig. 11-1. Use your level to check the floor and walls. Mark the locations of the bottom of the base cabinets and the top and bottom of the wall cabinets (Courtesy of Medallion Kitchens).

Store the cabinets in an out of the way place, like the garage, where they'll be safe and protected from the weather. Leave them crated for now, and unpack them as you bring them into the house. Inspect each one carefully for damage as you unpack them. If you discover any damage, repack the cabinet and notify your dealer immediately for a replacement. If the damage is to the door only, you can often still hang the cabinet itself while a replacement door is being ordered.

Using your long level, or a short level and a long, straight board, check the floor to see how level it is (Fig. 11-1). Check around the room in any area where cabinets will be installed, paying particular attention to the area between the wall and about 24 inches out. If there is a definite slope in the floor, which is common, determine where the highest point is. Working from this high point, strike a level line

on the wall around the room, using your level and a chalk line. This line, called the base line, indicates where the bottom of the base cabinets will rest and gives you an idea of where shimming will be needed and in what amount.

Next, if you haven't already done so, mark the actual cabinet locations on the walls (Fig. 11-2). Be accurate in your layout, and include any fillers you'll be using to make up odd inches. Pay particular attention to how the cabinets lay out around windows and doors, and adjust your fills accordingly.

Now check the walls for high spots, again using your long level or the board (Fig. 11-3). Place the board on edge against the wall and pivot it up and down, marking any spots that are obviously high or low with a pencil. Small irregularities are common, and can be dealt with with shims as the cabinets are installed. Deep low spots should be filled in now with

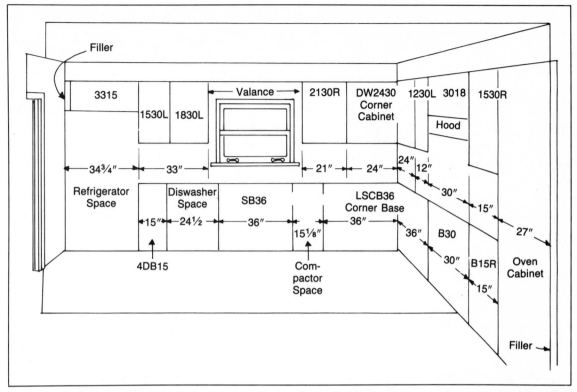

Fig. 11-2. Mark the locations of all the cabinets and fillers on the wall to check that your measurements equal the length of the wall (Courtesy of Medallion Kitchens).

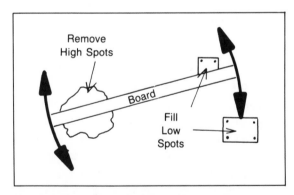

Fig. 11-3. Move a long, straight board across the wall to determine extreme high and low spots. Correct them before proceeding with the installation.

patching plaster or any suitable shimming material, and severe high spots should be sanded or scraped down to prevent problems later.

If your kitchen is utilizing tall units, such as oven or pantry cabinets, they will require a full 84 inches in height. At the location where each tall unit is to be installed, measure up from the base line (not the floor) 84 inches (Fig. 11-1), and mark the wall. Working from this point (or points) use your level and chalk line to mark a level line around the room. This line indicates where the top of the upper cabinets will be. If the room has an existing soffit and the height from the base line to the soffit is less than 84 inches, you will need to work to the soffit and trim off the bottom of the tall units to make the adjustment.

Take the time now to locate and mark the studs (Fig. 11-4). If you know the location of any studs from the rough work you did earlier, measure out on 16 inch centers to locate the rest of them. You can probe with a hammer and a small finish nail to verify the location. If you don't know the location of any of the studs, you can sound for them by tapping the wall with the handle of the hammer and listening for the solid area (this works fairly well on

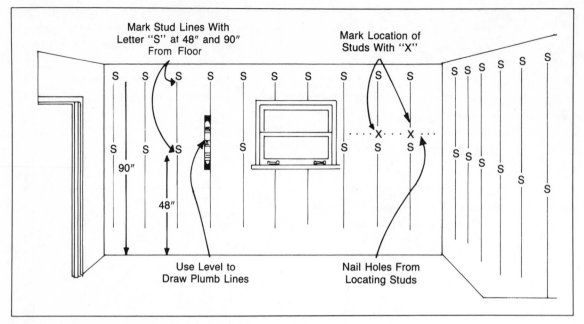

Fig. 11-4. Mark the stud locations on the walls for reference during installation (Courtesy of Medallion Kitchens).

drywall but not on plaster), or you can use a stud finder. Two types of stud finders are available; magnetic, which reacts to the nails in the studs, and the more expensive electronic models, which sense the change in density when a stud is located.

When you have the stud locations, mark them on the wall with a lumber crayon or a soft lead pencil. If you make the marks about 48 and 90 inches off the floor, they'll be visible for both the upper and the lower cabinets.

Finally, measure down from your upper line 30 inches and mark the wall. (Fig. 11-1). Double-check this point by measuring up from the base line; the measurement should be 54 inches. At this point, carefully level a length of 1 × 4 or other scrap lumber and mark the wall. If you wish, you can secure the 1 × 4 to the wall to act as a support, but the nail holes will need to be repaired if they're not being covered later by a back splash. Be sure the cleat is secured into the studs.

INSTALLING THE WALL CABINETS

Most carpenters prefer to begin by installing the wall cabinets. Where you choose to begin is up to you, but you may find it awkward working around the wider base cabinets to hang the wall units.

If you choose to begin with the base cabinets, you will need to either install the counters or cover the cabinets with temporary material, such as a sheet of plywood. This will give you a solid base to support the wall cabinets off of while they're being installed.

The First Corner Cabinet

Installation begins with a corner cabinet and works out from there. Select the first cabinet and place it in the corner, resting it on the wall cleat. If you are not using the wall cleat, you may wish to make a support to brace the cabinet.

If necessary, have a helper brace the cabinet while you check it for plumb and level. Wooden shims can be driven between the cabinet and the wall, as needed to bring the cabinet perfectly into position. Take your time, and check the cabinet with a level in several locations.

When the cabinet is properly positioned, drill through the upper and lower nailing strips inside the cabinet into the studs (Fig. 11-5). Using drywall

110

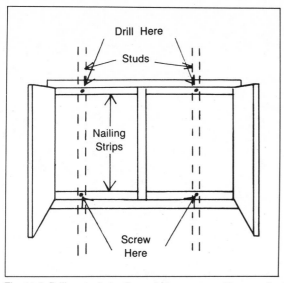

Fig. 11-5. Drill screw holes through the upper and lower nailing strips into the studs.

screws, or the specific screws recommended by the cabinet manufacturer, screw the cabinet snugly but not tightly against the wall. Final tightening of the screws will come later.

If you are using a blind corner cabinet (Fig. 11-6), it's important to pull the cabinet the proper distance, as called for in your layout. Measure this distance carefully, set the cabinet in place, then shim it plumb and level and screw it to the wall.

Fillers

Fillers are used to make up odd inches in a run of cabinets, and to adjust the *reveals* (that portion of wall that remains exposed) around windows and doors. They are cut from the same material that the cabinets are made from, and are the same thickness as the *cabinet stiles* (the vertical portions of the frame). Filler material that is prefinished to match the cabinets can be obtained from the manufacturer.

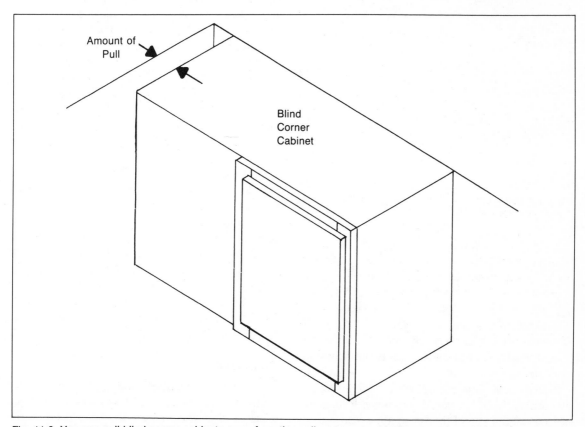

Fig. 11-6. You can pull blind corner cabinets away from the wall up to several inches to make up odd measurements.

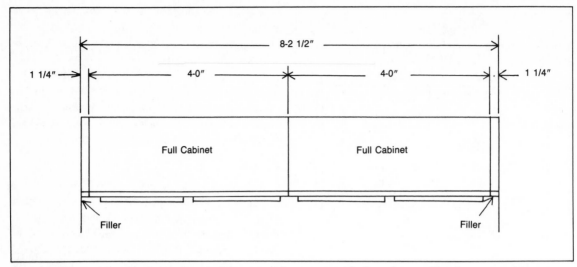

Fig. 11-7. Filler strips, placed at each end of the run, make up uneven inches when working from corner to corner.

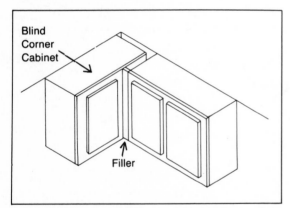

Fig. 11-8. Use fillers in corners to ensure that the cabinet doors have adequate room to swing.

As an example (Fig. 11-7), suppose you are installing cabinets on a wall that measures 8 feet 2½ inches from corner to corner. There are several combinations of cabinets that will equal 8 feet, leaving you with 2½ inches to fill. This filled-in area would normally be accomplished by splitting the fill between the two corners; rip two 1¼-inch strips from the fill stock and install them at the beginning and the end of the run.

In general, if the cabinet run goes from corner to corner, the fillers should be evenly divided and placed at each end of the run, rather than placing them in the middle or all at one end. For runs which

start in a corner and end at a window or door, place all the fills at the starting corner.

Filler strips are also used in corners (Fig. 11-8), to ensure that adequate clearance is provided for drawers to open, or for cabinet or appliance doors to swing. The need for fillers will vary with the size of the cabinet's faceframe and the depth of the handles you're using. You'll need to make that determination as you go along.

Filler strips are installed on the cabinet before the cabinet is put into place (Fig. 11-9). Rip the filler to the proper width, then cut its length to match the height of the cabinet. Place the filler next to the appropriate stile, carefully align the bottoms and the faces, and hold the filler in place with C or bar clamps. Drill a pilot hole through the edge of the filler about halfway into the stile, countersink the hole and secure the filler with drywall screws. Place two screws from the filler into the cabinet, about 3 inches down from the top and 3 inches up from the bottom. Place a third screw in the center, from the cabinet into the filler.

Continuing the Run

With the first corner cabinet and any necessary fillers in place, the second wall cabinet in the run is placed in position next to the first. Set it on the cleat or otherwise prop it into place, then carefully

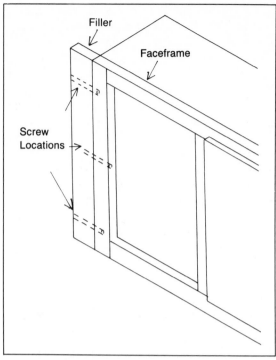

Fig. 11-9. Carefully align and secure the fillers to the cabinet before the cabinet is put into place.

align it with the first cabinet. When the bottoms and faces of the stiles are flush, use your C-clamps to clamp the two cabinets together (Fig. 11-10). Connect the cabinets as you did the filler, with two screws in from one side at the top and bottom and one in from the other side in the center.

When the cabinets are secured to each other, check the second cabinet for plumb and level, and shim it as necessary. Drill through the upper and lower nailing strips into the studs and screw the cabinet to the wall. Once again, do not fully tighten the screws.

Install each subsequent cabinet in order; connect the stiles, shim the cabinet, and secure it to the wall. When you reach the end of one entire run, check the run using a long level, or a 2-foot level placed on a long straight board. Double check each cabinet for plumb, and check the alignment of the doors. When everything looks correct, finish tightening the screws.

Subsequent wall cabinet runs are installed in the same manner, working out from the first corner. Finish installing all the wall cabinets before beginning the base runs.

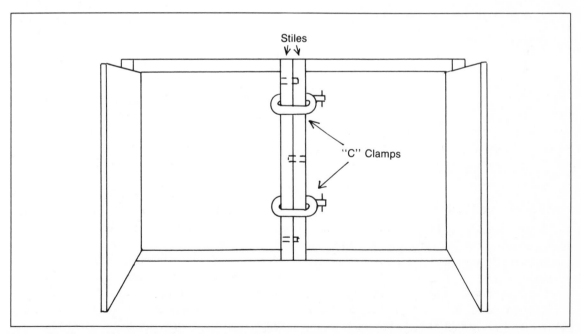

Fig. 11-10. Align and clamp adjacent cabinets with C-clamps, then secure them with screws driven in from each side.

Fig. 11-11. Shims are necessary above cabinets with thin tops to provide adequate support before hanging the cabinet from the ceiling.

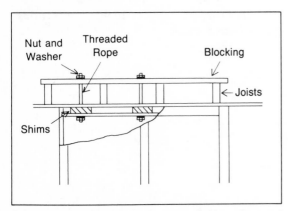

Fig. 11-12. Place threaded rods, secured with washers and nuts, through the cabinets into a board laid across the joist when additional load support is necessary.

Ceiling-Mounted Cabinets

It may be necessary to hang a cabinet from the ceiling, such as over a peninsula. In this case, the cabinet needs to be secured up into the ceiling joists, or into appropriate blocking.

If the top of the cabinet has been constructed from ¾ inch or thicker material, you can screw directly through the top. First, locate and mark the joists as you did for the studs. Drill a pilot hole through the top into the joist, countersink it, and secure the cabinet with long drywall screws. Install the screws on 16-inch centers to ensure good support.

For thinner tops, you'll need to place backing material on top of the cabinet before it's installed (Fig. 11-11), to prevent distorting the cabinet top and to provide adequate strength. Measure from the top to the upper edge of the faceframe, and install shims of the appropriate thickness before screwing the cabinet into place.

For additional strength, you may wish to bolt the cabinet in place (Fig. 11-12). Bolting is done by first drilling up through the cabinet, through the ceiling, and through blocking placed over the tops of the joists. Next, insert ⅜- or ½-inch-diameter threaded rod through the holes, and secure it with a nut and washer at each end. If the top of the cabinet is less than ¾ inch thick, install backing material.

INSTALLING THE BASE CABINETS

Begin laying out the base cabinets from one corner. Since support is not a problem for the base cabinets, you'll usually find it easiest to bring in all the cabinets for one run and set them together. If there is a tall unit at the end of the run, set that in position also. Carefully align the tall unit with the upper cabinets, shim it so it's plumb, then work back from it to the corner to get the exact sizes of any fills you'll need (Fig. 11-13).

Attach the stiles of the base cabinets together, using the same methods used for the wall cabinets. Carefully align the bottoms and faces of the stiles, and clamp the cabinets together. Drill and countersink the holes, and secure the cabinets by placing a top and bottom screw from one side and a center screw from the other.

If you have a blind corner cabinet (Fig. 11-14), pull it out the appropriate distance to make up the odd inches. If you are starting with a lazy-Susan cabinet (Fig. 11-15), pull it out from the wall to whatever distance is recommended by the manufacturer (usually 36 inches), then make up any odd inches using fillers. With the lazy-Susan cabinet, you'll also need to place some 1 × 3 cleats in the corner to support the countertop, and this is easier to do before the cabinets go in. Measure up the appropriate

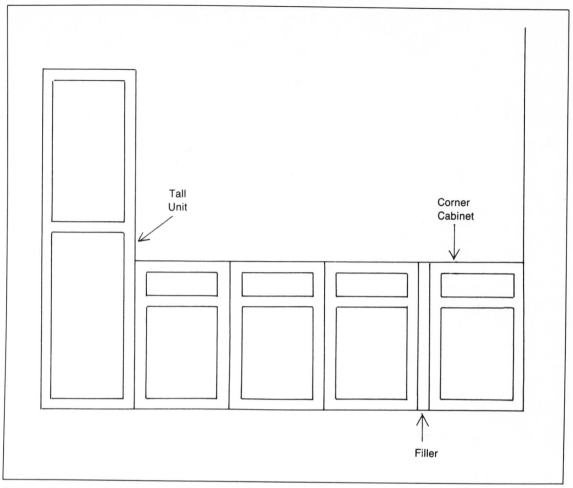

Fig. 11-13. Set tall units in place and plumb them in order to be able to measure back to the corner and verify the width of any fillers.

distance, level the cleats, and screw or nail them to the studs.

When the entire run is connected and flush against the wall, use your long level and check the run. Starting from the high point, drive shims between the cabinet and the floor to raise the entire run level. Next, check each cabinet for plumb, and shim it away from the wall as necessary to bring it plumb. Place the shims where the studs are so that the cabinet's screws will hold them in place.

When the run is plumb and level, screw through the back of the cabinets into the studs. If the run is especially long, you may wish to shim the cabinets as you go and hold them with a screw in every

third or fourth stud, then go back and level and secure the entire run.

Tall units need to be secured to both the upper and lower cabinets by carefully aligning the stiles and then screwing through the faceframes. If you are installing the tall unit next to a 12-inch-deep wall cabinet, screw through the side of the tall unit into the stile of the wall cabinet.

Aligning the Runs to Each Other

When all of the base runs are installed and leveled, adjacent L- or U-shaped runs need to be checked in relation to each other. This is an impor-

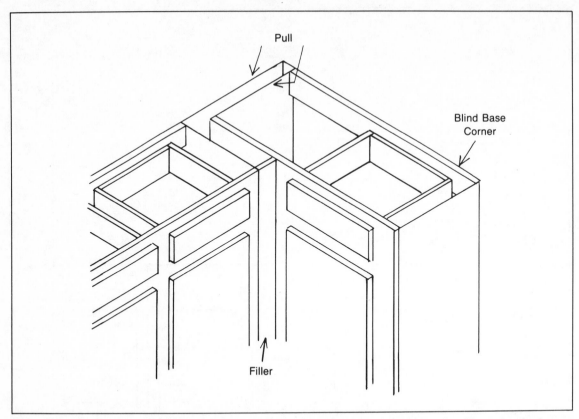

Fig. 11-14. As with the wall cabinets, pull blind base corners to make up uneven inches, and use a filler so that the drawers can open without hitting the adjacent handles. Use of corner fills will vary with the installation and the type of handles being used.

tant step both for appearance and for proper alignment of the countertops.

First, check to see if the runs are square to each other (Fig. 11-16). Preliminary checking can be done with a framing square as the cabinets are being installed, after which you'll want to check them using the 3:4:5 method.

Measure 3 feet out from the corner along one run and make a mark, and 4 feet out from the corner along the second run. If the distance between the two marks is exactly 5 feet, the runs are square. If not, move them in or out by shimming until the measurement is correct.

Next, place a long, straight board across between the runs (Fig. 11-17), and check to see if they are level to each other. If not, adjust them by shimming.

Dishwasher and Refrigerator Panels

If the dishwasher, refrigerator, or trash compactor is to be placed at the end of a run, a panel needs to be installed to finish off the run and protect the appliances. Dishwasher panels, also used next to a trash compactor, are 34½ inches high and 24 inches wide. Most have a 1 × 2 attached to the front to create a finished edge, and some have a toe kick cutout. Refrigerator panels (Fig. 11-18), which are sometimes used alongside oven and pantry cabinets, are 84 inches high and 24 inches deep. Once again, most have a finished front edge.

The panels are installed as the cabinets are being placed, and before the appliances are installed. The dishwasher panel is secured to the floor and to the back wall. If it falls between studs, you may need to use toggle bolts or molly bolts to hold it in place.

116

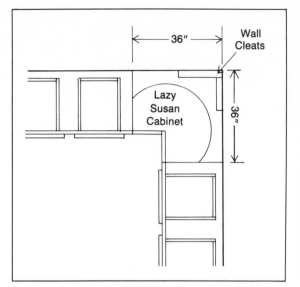

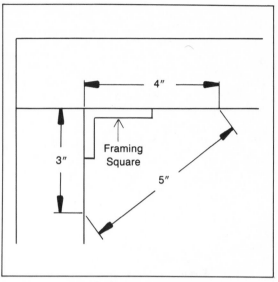

Fig. 11-15. The lazy-Susan cabinet needs to be pulled away from the wall in both directions in order to align with the face of both runs. Wall cleats in the corner support the countertop.

Fig. 11-16. Use a framing square and the simple 3:4:5 method to check that L- and U-shaped runs are square to each other.

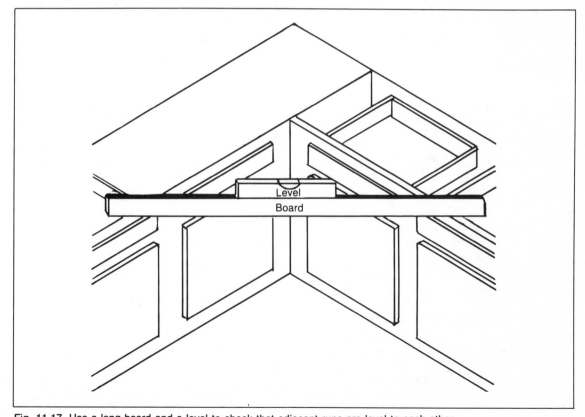

Fig. 11-17. Use a long board and a level to check that adjacent runs are level to each other.

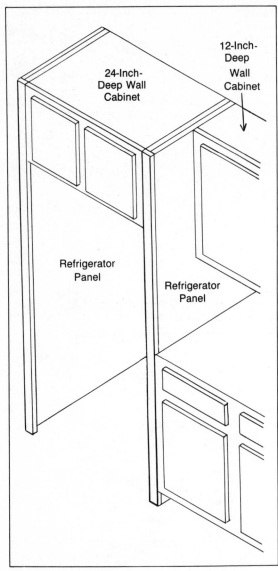

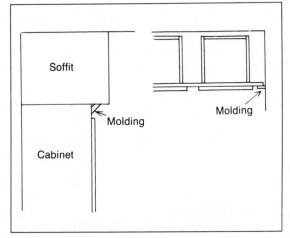

close up any gaps. Prefinished moldings can usually be obtained from the same manufacturer that supplied the cabinets, or you can purchase any molding you like and stain or paint it to match.

Moldings should be applied where the wall cabinets meet the soffit or ceiling, and where the wall and base cabinets meet the walls (Fig. 11-19). Cut off all overhanging shims first, then scribe the molding to match to any irregularities in the wall for a clean fit. The moldings can be installed with finish nails which are colored to match the finish, or with regular finish nails that are then countersunk and puttied over.

For wall cabinets that do not have a soffit above them, various railings are available that provide a nice finished look. You can use a crown molding that extends up above the cabinets, or a spindle rail that is mounted on top of the cabinets.

INSTALLING EUROPEAN-STYLE CABINETS

A new style of cabinetry which is becoming quite popular is the European-style cabinet. Characterized by clean lines and a number of innovative options, these cabinets have no faceframe in the conventional sense. The cabinet is essentially an open-fronted box with large doors and drawers that cover the entire front. Multiadjustable concealed hinges and built-in pulls complete the clean lines.

Fig. 11-18. Two refrigerator panels being used to create an alcove for the refrigerator. This type of installation requires the use of a 24-inch-deep cabinet over the refrigerator, which is handy for tray storage.

L-brackets will work well to hold it to the floor. The refrigerator panel is secured to the upper cabinets, to the floor, and sometimes to the wall, also.

TRIMMING OUT

The final professional touch for your cabinet installation is to use moldings to highlight the cabinets and

Fig. 11-19. Molding being used at the soffit and along the wall to finish off the cabinet installation.

Installation procedures for some of these cabinets are a little different from conventional cabinets, and will vary among manufacturers. Refer to the manufacturer's instructions for specific details.

In general, the wall cabinets are mounted on a wall track. The track is leveled and screwed to the studs, then the cabinets are hung on the track. Adjustments in the hanging clips allow the cabinets to be raised or lowered to level them.

Some styles of base cabinets have exposed screw legs, which simplifies leveling. After the cabinets have been leveled and screwed to the wall, the toe kick cover panel is simply snapped in place to provide a very clean, finished look.

Both upper and lower cabinets are screwed to each other as conventional cabinets are, but the screw heads are recessed and then concealed with decorative snap-on tops that match the surrounding laminate finish. Final adjustment of the lines is done with the hinges, which can move the doors up, down, in and out, and side to side for perfect alignment.

Chapter 12

Topping Off the Counters

A S YOUR PLANS PROGRESS FOR YOUR KITCHEN, you'll probably find yourself confronted with a much wider choice of countertop materials than you had thought were available. Synthetic materials, natural materials, blends—there's quite a choice. Add the possibilities of mixing different materials in the same kitchen, and the combinations seem endless.

This chapter will begin with a look at some of the different materials that are available and what their relative advantages and disadvantages are. The rest of the chapter will concentrate on installation procedures for the two most popular—ceramic tile and plastic laminates.

COUNTERTOP MATERIALS

There are many countertop materials available, and the choice needs to be made on the basis of appearance, practicality, and cost. Special-purpose countertop material can be used in small quantities with other materials to keep costs down, or two or more materials may be blended for decorative effect.

Plastic Laminates

Plastic laminates are probably the most common of all the countertop materials. Plastic laminates are comprised of a decorative paper that is bonded to several layers of resin-treated kraft paper, then covered with a translucent, melamine-resin paper that becomes clear during processing. The laminate material is then bonded to plywood or particleboard to form a countertop.

Laminate counters are available in hundreds of colors and patterns, and the countertop itself may take one of several forms (Fig. 12-1). These types of counters are about the easiest for the do-it-yourselfer to work with, and are also among the least expensive. They are quite easy to care for, are resistant to water, alcohol, stains, and most common chemicals, and are durable.

The biggest disadvantage to plastic laminate is that it's not resistant to heat. Setting a hot pot on the counter can cause a permanent burn mark. As a precaution when using this type of counter, you should plan on having a fixed or portable section of tile or other heatproof material near the cooktop to receive hot pots and pans. Plastic laminate can also chip if struck hard enough, and the pattern wears off on some of the older styles. This problem has mostly been eliminated with today's harder coatings and deeper color layers.

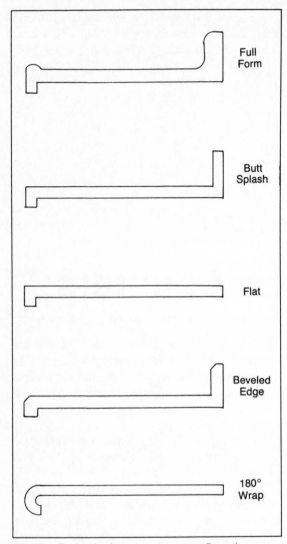

Fig. 12-1. Typical laminate countertop configurations.

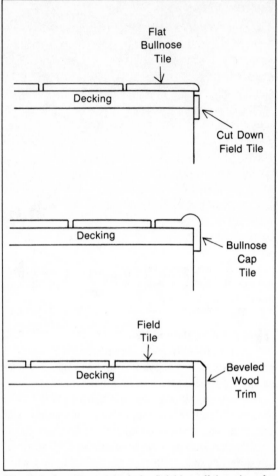

Fig. 12-2. Common methods for finishing off the edge of a ceramic tile countertop.

Ceramic Tile

For years, ceramic tile was virtually the only countertop material found in the kitchen. It was gradually replaced by plastic laminates as cost became a factor, but is enjoying a revival of popularity. For elegance and durability, few countertop materials can touch tile.

Ceramic tile is available glazed or unglazed, but only glazed materials should be used on countertops. A limitless assortment of colors, styles and patterns are available, along with decorative tiles that have colorful pictures and patterns on them, for use as border or accent tiles. A variety of edge treatments are also used (Fig. 12-2).

Ceramic tile is nearly indestructible in normal use, although a sharp, hard blow can crack or chip the tile. It is resistant to just about everything, including water, alcohol, and common chemicals, and is not affected by direct heat.

Problems with the tiles themselves are rare—most tile countertop problems stem from improper installation of the underlying decking material. The grout lines on the tile present a cleaning problem for some people, which can be minimized by using wider grout spacing and sealing the grout lines.

Butcher Block

Butcher block counters have several advantages. Constructed of maple, alder, or other hardwood, they're almost completely indestructible, and even after years of use they can be renewed by sanding or planing. They offer an excellent surface for pastries and are often sought after by the gourmet cook and baker. Factory applied, nontoxic finishes are also available that are not affected by cutting or chopping operations, and that are safe for contact with food.

Cost and upkeep are the two major drawbacks. Doing an entire kitchen with real butcher block counters can be quite expensive when compared with other materials, and unfinished blocks require weekly cleaning and finishing with mineral oil. They are not as resistant to spills as tile, and while they will withstand some contact with heat, prolonged contact can cause burn marks.

Corian

Corian is the brand name of a tough, rigid, transparent acrylic polymer material created by DuPont. It offers a number of advantages for the kitchen, and has become increasingly popular in recent years. Corian is very easy to care for, smooth, extremely durable, and resistant to water, heat, and staining. Certain chemicals, such as nail polish remover and acidic drain cleaners, can cause damage. The color is blended completely through the material, so most damage can be repaired with a light sanding using 320-grit sandpaper.

Corian is available in several colors, although the choices are not nearly as wide as with tile or laminates, which may be a drawback in some color schemes. Costs vary, but most installations are approximately 1½ to 2 times as expensive as a mortar-base ceramic tile installation.

Natural Stone

Natural stone materials like marble, granite, slate, and others have all found their way onto kitchen counters over the years, and they offer some very distinct advantages and disadvantages.

For the avid baker, few materials compare with a natural stone surface. It is cool, smooth, and unsurpassed for working with various doughs. Candy making is another kitchen specialty it's especially suited for. Marble in particular is found on at least one counter in many fine bakeries and candy stores.

Cost is probably the biggest disadvantage to these types of counters. Depending on the size, quality and thickness of the stone slabs that are quarried for the counter, they can range from moderately to extremely expensive. They are also out of the range of the do-it-yourselfer, requiring specialized tools and skills for proper installation. Maintenance and upkeep can also be a problem. They're definitely not the counter of choice for an active family with several children.

The best solution for most kitchens is compromise. You might consider a slab of marble or other material as a counter for your baking center, or even as just an insert in that counter, while going with ceramic tile or other complementary countertop surfaces in the rest of the kitchen.

INSTALLING A PLASTIC LAMINATE COUNTER

Plastic laminate counters are probably the easiest of all the countertop materials for the do-it-yourselfer to work with. Most of the work will already have been done for you by the time you pick up the counters.

You will mostly need just basic hand tools for the installation, including a screwdriver, measuring tape, open-end wrench, a compass, and perhaps a file. In addition, you'll need a hand or electric drill with assorted bits and an electric jig saw or a keyhole saw for making cutouts, plus a circular saw with a fine-toothed plywood blade or a hand saw with 10 to 12 teeth per inch if you need to cut the counters to length.

Measuring

The critical step with laminate counters is the measuring. If possible, it's best to wait until the base cabinets are installed before taking measurements. If your dealer has a backlog, however, this may cause a delay of several days in the installation, so you may have no choice but to make the order beforehand. In either case, measure the kitchen very carefully, especially from corner to corner and up to window and door openings. If you are having the cutouts done for you, they'll need to know the exact location and sizes of the sink, cooktop, range, etc.

Make a complete sketch of the kitchen, and write in all the dimensions. When you're done, measure the kitchen a second time to verify the measurements. Remember, if the countertop is made even slightly too short, it's no good to you, and you're out the cost of it. You may want to check with your dealer about measuring. In many cases they will send an estimator out to take their own measurements.

Cutting the Countertop

You'll want to order your counters to exact size to minimize cutting on the job site. If this is not possible, order the counters long and cut them after the cabinets are in and you're able to verify the measurements.

Place the countertop on a stable surface, such as two sawhorses, and mark the length on the counter in pencil. Place a strip of masking tape over the pencil marks, then remeasure and mark directly on the tape. Using a framing square for accuracy, draw the cutting line on the tape.

If you are using a handsaw for the cut, cut from the top side of the counter. Cut on the outside of the pencil line, directly through the masking tape, starting from the backsplash and working to the front. To minimize the chances of chipping the laminate, cut slowly and apply pressure on the down stroke of the saw only.

With a circular saw, jig saw, or any saw that cuts on the up stroke, you'll be making the cut from the back side, with the counter upside down. Mark your cutting line on the back. Be sure to put a piece of masking tape over the line of cut on the front side (tape is not necessary on the back). After cutting with any type of saw, finish off the cut edge with a fine file or a sanding block and 30 grit sandpaper.

To make cutouts for the sink, cooktop, or other appliances, the cutting procedure is essentially the same. Cutouts can be made with the counters out and sitting on sawhorses, or after the counters have been installed, provided there is enough clearance within the cabinet for the saw blade to move.

Carefully measure and mark the cutout, using the sink rim, a template, or the manufacturer's instructions to establish the exact size. Remember to double check your measurements before beginning the cut. Use a center punch and make an indentation in one corner, then drill through the countertop. Use a ¾ inch bit, or any bit that's large enough for your saw blade.

Handsaw cuts can be made from the top side, while jig saw or other power saw cuts should be made from underneath for best results. Good results can still be achieved when using a power saw from the top of the counter. Use a fine-toothed blade, and cut slowly. Let the saw do the work without forcing the cut. As an added precaution against chipping, you may wish to place transparent tape over your pencil lines, and cut directly through the tape. When the cut is finished, smooth the edges with a file or sandpaper.

Assembling the Counter

When the cuts are complete, the counters can be assembled. If you are using end caps to cover an exposed end, first install wood strips of the appropriate size under the counter to serve as backing for the cap. Install the end caps with contact cement, taking care to align them correctly with the contours of the counter. Use a file or sanding block to remove excess glue and smooth the lines after installation.

Test fit one of the counters to be certain the overhanging front lip doesn't interfere with the drawers or undercounter appliances. If it does, you'll need to install spacer blocks to raise the counter the appropriate distance. These spacer blocks can be installed directly on the underside of the counters with glue and screws or nails, or you can install strips of wood on top of the cabinets.

If you have a mitered corner or other area

where two counters will be joined to each other, you will notice that the dealer has made a series of slotted cutouts on the underside of the counter. You will also be supplied with a number of special T-bolts for use in assembling the joint.

Turn the counters upside down on sawhorses or other stable support. Coat the edges of the joint with a waterproof, plastic resin glue (your dealer can supply you with the appropriate glue), then butt the two sections together. Insert the T-bolts into the slots. Carefully align the top faces of the sections, and secure them by tightening the bolts. Nail the backsplashes together from the back side, also. If you have installed blocks to raise the height of the counter, install some along the mitered joints for additional support, or provide backing under the joint on top of the cabinets.

Installing the Counters

Bring the assembled counters into the kitchen and set them in place on the cabinets. (If you are assembling the counters outside, be certain you have enough clearance through doorways to bring them in. If not, assemble them in the kitchen.) Carefully align them to the cabinets at the wall.

If the counters do not fit snugly against the wall, you will need to scribe them. Pull them away from the wall about ¼ inch, and carefully align them so they are parallel with the front of the cabinets. Set your compass to the greatest distance away from the wall. With the compass point against the wall, move the compass carefully down the wall and mark the top of the backsplash with the pencil point. Use a block plane or a mill file to file the counter down to your line.

You may wish to purchase your counters without a backsplash, then use ceramic tile to create an attractive partial or full splash. If you are using tile on the backsplash, be certain the laminate counter fits close enough to the back wall so that the thickness of the tile will cover any gaps.

When the counters are correctly in place, secure them by driving screws up through the blocking in the corners of the cabinets and into the underside of the counters. Be certain your screws

are long enough to penetrate well into the counter, but not all the way through.

INSTALLING A CERAMIC TILE COUNTER

The methods and materials for installing ceramic tile have been simplified to the point where many installations can be handled with good results by the patient do-it-yourselfer. Solid decking and careful planning and layout are the keys, along with selecting the proper materials for your particular job.

For many years, the standard installation method was to first lay a thick, level mortar base, allow it to dry, then adhere the tile to that (Figs. 12-5 to 12-14). This procedure is still the method preferred by professional tile setters, but perfectly acceptable results can be obtained working with adhesive over a plywood base (Figs. 12-15 to 12-24).

Decking for Tile

The wood base installed over the top of the base cabinets that the tile rests on is called the *deck*, and its proper installation is essential for a good tile job. Most failures in a finished tile installation can be traced back to a failure in the decking.

For a mortar base installation, the decking is done with 1-×-4 or 1-×-6 Douglas fir (Fig. 12-3). Select #1 or #2 grade boards that are straight, dry, clean, and relatively free of defects. Try to have the decking material on the job several days in advance, so that it can season and adjust to the room.

The decking boards can be applied either parallel or perpendicular to the face of the cabinets, with a spacing of about ¼ inch between the boards. Fasten the boards securely to the tops of the cabinets, using screws (preferred) or ring shank nails.

Plywood should be avoided as a decking under mortar-base tile, but its use is necessary in some cases, such as on wide overhangs and eating counters. If plywood is necessary for your installation, use ¾-inch exterior grade, either A-C or C-C Plugged and Sanded. After the plywood is installed, make a regular series of saw kerfs (Fig. 12-4), all the way through the plywood to allow it to expand and contract under the tile.

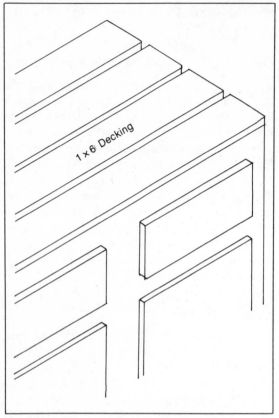

Fig. 12-3. Use 1×6 lumber over the base cabinets to provide a deck for the installation of ceramic tile.

For an installation using mastic on plywood, the cabinets should be decked with ¾-inch A-C or C-C Plugged and Sanded plywood. Use exterior grade plywood only, not interior grade, particle board, or any other material. If the cabinets were installed correctly, the plywood top should be level. If it isn't, shims can be placed on top of the cabinets to level the decking.

Test fit a piece of cap tile on the front edge of the plywood to be certain drawers and appliances will clear the tile. If they don't, block under the plywood as necessary to raise it. Secure the plywood with screws or ring shank nails. Make a few random saw kerfs in the plywood to allow for expansion and contraction.

Make all necessary cutouts in the decking for sinks and appliances, and test fit them for accuracy. Double check that the decking is level and secure, and that the cut ends of the decking around any openings are adequately supported to carry the weight of the sink or appliance.

Laying Out the Tile

Dry fit the tile on the decking before installation. Begin by placing cap tiles over the front, and work from front to back with full tiles. A wooden front trim board can be used in place of the cap tile,

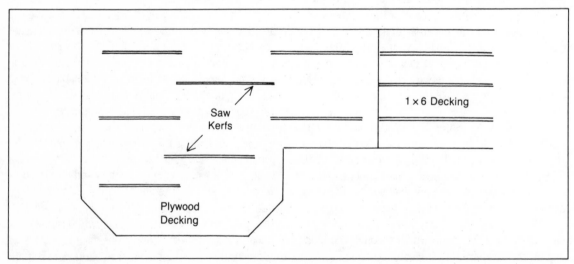

Fig. 12-4. Cut saw kerfs into plywood countertop decking to relieve stain and prevent movement that could crack the tile.

Fig. 12-5. Cover the decking with 15-pound felt to seal against moisture. The felt should extend up the sidewalls at least 2 inches (Courtesy of American Olean Tile).

Fig. 12-6. Place a metal lath over the felt next to provide a base for the mortar (Courtesy of American Olean Tile).

Fig. 12-7. A punched metal strip is attached to the front of the decking and leveled at the height that the mortar will be applied (Courtesy of American Olean Tile).

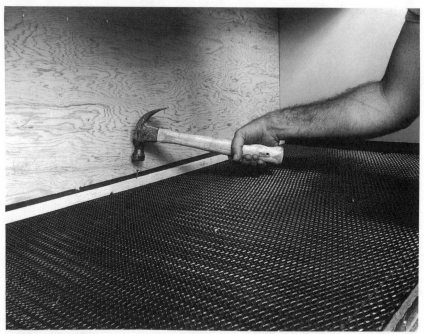

Fig. 12-8. At the back of the counter, attach a screed strip. The strip is the same height as the front metal (Courtesy of American Olean Tile).

128

Fig. 12-9. Spread the mortar and compact it over the metal lath to height just above the screed strip and the front metal (Courtesy of American Olean Tile).

Fig. 12-10. With a back and forth motion, use a straight board to screed off the excess mortar and level the entire counter (Courtesy of American Olean Tile).

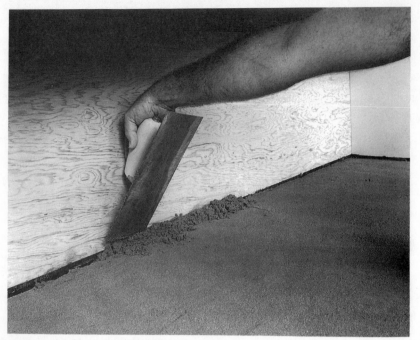

Fig. 12-11. As the mortar begins to set, remove the screed strip and use fresh mortar to fill in the resulting hole flush with the surrounding deck (Courtesy of American Olean Tile).

Fig. 12-12. Lay out the cap tiles and field tiles to determine tne best location for the cuts. Use ¼-inch plastic spacers to create uniform spacing between the tiles (Courtesy of American Olean Tile).

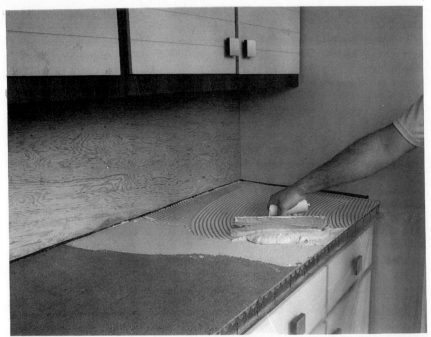

Fig. 12-13. Apply mortar over the dried bed using a ¼-×-¼ notched trowel (Courtesy of American Olean Tile).

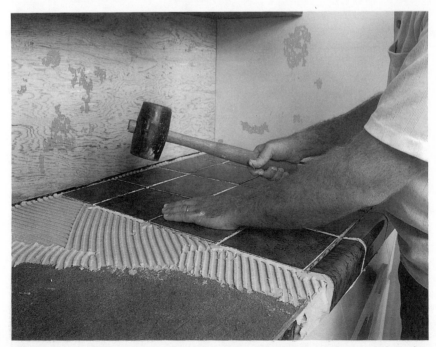

Fig. 12-14. Cut the tiles as needed and set them into the mortar, using the spacers for consistency. Leave the spacers in place and later grout them over. Use a rubber mallet to gently tap the tiles into full contact with the mortar. After the tiles are dry, grouting proceeds the same as for mastic tile (Courtesy of American Olean Tile).

Fig. 12-15. Carefully lay out the tiles to determine the best location for the cuts (Courtesy of American Olean Tile).

Fig. 12-16. Cover the ¾-inch plywood deck with mastic using a ³⁄₁₆-inch-notched trowel (Courtesy of American Olean Tile).

Fig. 12-17. Lay out the tiles and press them into the mastic. Make cuts as necessary around the sink and other openings (Courtesy of American Olean Tile).

Fig. 12-18. Apply tile to the backsplash. Make your cuts in the row directly up under the wall cabinets, since these will be the least conspicuous (Courtesy of American Olean Tile).

Fig. 12-19. Use bullnose tile to finish off the sidewall installation, creating a smooth, rounded edge (Courtesy of American Olean Tile).

Fig. 12-20. Grouting procedures are the same for mastic or mortared tile. Wait at least 24 hours for the tile to set up, then apply the grout with a rubber grouting trowel. Work the grout diagonally across the grout lines to fill them completely (Courtesy of American Olean Tile).

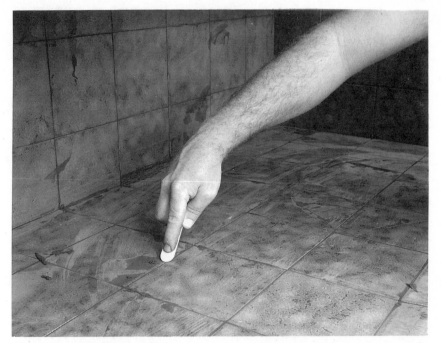

Fig. 12-21. Strike the joints with a tongue depresser or similar object to make them dense, smooth and uniform. This step makes the grout easier to clean in the future (Courtesy of American Olean Tile).

Fig. 12-22. Use a damp sponge to wipe off the excess grout, rinsing the sponge frequently in clean water (Courtesy of American Olean Tile).

Fig. 12-23. After the grout has dried to a haze, about 24 hours, thoroughly wipe the tile with a soft, dry cloth. Lightly buff the tile to a shine (Courtesy of American Olean Tile).

Fig. 12-24. The completed installation. Ceramic tile makes a beautiful, durable counter that will compliment the kitchen decor for many years (Courtesy of American Olean Tile).

if desired. In this case, begin with full tiles at the front edge of the counter, and install the board after the installation is complete.

Working from front to back, the cut tiles will be the last row, with the cut edge against the back wall. Work down the counter with full tiles, and see how they lay out around the sink and up against windows.

Sinks are often centered under the window, so if you center the tile to the sink, it will be centered to the window as well. It will usually look best if the tile is centered on the sink or window, then worked out from there so that any cuts are made at the ends of the counters. Experiment with several different layouts of the tile and spacing for the grout lines, until you have one that you like the appearance of. Grout lines can be as thin as $\frac{1}{16}$ inch up to $\frac{3}{8}$ inch or more. Generally, thin lines look best with small tile, while $\frac{1}{4}$-inch lines nicely complement larger tiles, such as 6-inch square.

Laying the Tile

Clean the plywood thoroughly and remove all dust. Using a notched trowel with a notch pattern that follows the adhesive manufacturer's recommendations, apply adhesive to the decking. Cover an area of about 8 to 10 square feet at a time with adhesive.

Following your layout pattern, place full cap tiles on the front of the decking, then proceed to work back toward the wall with full tiles. Some tiles have lugs cast into the edges of them for spacing. Abut the lugs and the spacing will be accurate. If the tile you're using does not have space lugs, or if you wish a wider grout line, you'll need to space the tile by hand. Small plastic spacers are the fastest and easiest method of accurate spacing.

As you reach the areas that are smaller than a full tile, cutting will be necessary. Hand tile cutters can be borrowed or rented from your tile dealer. If you have a number of cuts, especially intricate angles, or if you're working with a particularly hard or thick tile, you may wish to rent an electric, water-cooled tile saw from a rental yard. Make your cuts as you proceed, filling in all the spaces in the area where you've applied adhesive.

When the counters are done, proceed to the backsplash. Apply the adhesive in the same manner, and work up from the counter with full tiles. Take care to align the backsplash so that the grout lines are aligned to the countertop tiles.

If you are using a full backsplash, which is the most common, install full tiles until you reach the upper cabinets, then place the cut tiles up against the cabinets where they'll be less conspicuous. If you are using less than a full backsplash, install one or two rows of full tiles, making certain the last row has a rounded edge, called a bullnose. Where the cabinets meet a wall, a tile backsplash is usually installed on the side wall also. If desired, tile can also be installed on the side of a refrigerator panel.

Check the entire installation to be certain no excess adhesive has squeezed up above the tile. Allow the installation to dry for at least 24 hours so that the adhesive can set up before applying the grout.

Grouting the Tile

Applying grout is the last step in the installation. Select a grout color that is compatible with the color of the tile.

Mix the grout according to the manufacturer's instructions. Using a rubber float, apply the grout to the tile, working diagonally across the tile to be certain all the gaps are completely filled. Use the float to wipe off the excess, then strike the joints with a tongue depressor or similarly shaped object. This compresses and shapes the grout, making it easier to clean in the future.

Wipe the tile off with a damp sponge, rinsing it frequently in clean water. Allow the grout to dry for 12 to 24 hours, until a haze forms over the tile. Thoroughly clean the haze off the tiles with a lightly dampened sponge, then buff the tile dry and shiny with a soft cloth.

Chapter 13

Coloring the Kitchen

GONE FOREVER ARE THE DAYS OF THE DRAB, ALL white kitchen! Bright, bold and colorfully coordinated looks are becoming more and more a part of today's kitchen, and almost as much thought goes into the colors as into the cabinet layout.

The look of the kitchen, like the layout and the other elements of the design, should reflect you and your lifestyle. Casual, cozy, traditional, or formal, the overall theme of the kitchen is a big part of its appeal. And how it looks has a tremendous impact on how much you enjoy working there.

A COORDINATED LOOK

Early in your planning, you may want to consider giving the kitchen a coordinated look, or design motif, that is special and unique—something suited to you and your home. You may wish to carry out the look of the rest of the house, early American or Spanish for example, or create a room that's unique in its own right. Here are some looks you might want to consider for your kitchen:

☐ Modern: The modern kitchen features frameless cabinetry in bold colors, with vivid wall coverings and flooring. Chrome and stainless steel are used for accents and hardware. Stripes of color can also be used, for example a wide, bright orange line across white cabinets and up onto the wall. Foil wallcoverings work well in this type of room.

☐ Colonial: Colonial kitchens feature a more rustic and traditional look. Cabinetry is raised panel, natural wood in medium tones of color. Maple works especially well. You might consider ceiling beams made up from finished wood, with crown moldings at the ceiling line and around soffits. The wood moldings give a finish to the room like fine furniture. An open fireplace in brick will compliment the room also, as do exposed spice racks and cooking implements.

☐ European (Fig. 13-1): This is a relatively new look and it gets its name from the style of cabinetry first developed in Europe. The cabinets are frameless, with laminate coverings on the insides of the cases. The doors are laminate, often with real wood trim. Built-in features abound in these kitchens, and they are usually models of efficiency. The overall look is clean and uncluttered, with soft creams and almonds and occasional splashes of stained oak and bright accent colors for contrast.

☐ Mediterranean: The Mediterranean look centers around white stuccoed or heavily plastered walls and heavy, rough, dark stained ceiling beams. The overall look of the room is rustic and heavy. Dark cabinets are common against the white walls, and the hardware and accents can be of black wrought iron or dull pewter. Wall sconces, heavy hanging utensils, and other decorating features help set the mood of the room. Accent colors are usually bright red and olive green.

☐ Spanish Mission (Fig. 13-2): This type of kitchen is similar to the Mediterranean style, but somewhat less heavy. Gold and dull red tile is used extensively, as is adobe brick. Medium tones are good in the cabinets, and accent colors of bright yellow and green work well.

☐ Formal: Formal kitchens in the Empire or Federal styles typically have a rather reserved feeling. The cabinets can be of medium dark to dark tone, or painted in cream colors with muted accent colors in the moldings. The hardware should have an elegant look, usually in brass or gold.

☐ Country (Fig. 13-3): Casual is the key word for the country kitchen. It's typically open and airy, with lots of natural light. Cabinets should be light to medium in tone, in pine or oak. Leaving the cabinets open on top with a galley rail allows you to display antiques and other collectibles. Pale blues, yellows and greens make nice accent colors.

☐ Oriental: The traditional Oriental colors work best in this type of kitchen. A nice look combines polished black cabinets with red accents and polished brass hardware. Moldings on the cabinet doors and ornamental hardware strengthen the feeling.

Fig. 13-1. The "European" look, featuring clean lines and frameless cabinetry (Courtesy of Kitchen Kompact).

OVERCOMING A ROOM'S SHORTCOMINGS

With the right decorating, many of a room's short-comings can be overcome. Study the room carefully, and take note of anything you feel is a problem; a tall or short ceiling, an area that's too bright in the afternoon, a room that's too wide or too narrow. Make a list, and try some of these decorating tricks to fool the eye:

☐ Tall ceilings: Soffits with horizontal striped wall-paper can bring a ceiling down, as can massive beams. A darker, warm-toned color on the ceil-ing, even down to the tops of the wall cabinets, will also help.

☐ Short ceiling: If your kitchen has a short ceiling, the opposite tricks will work. Beams should be small and widely spaced if used at all, and should be painted white or stained a light color. Verti-cal stripes on the soffits help, and the ceiling should be white or a light, cool color.

☐ Narrow room: Horizontal stripes on the wall-covering will widen a narrow room. If the room feels long and narrow, try a warm, fairly dark paint or wallcovering on the narrow wall.

☐ Small room: Bright and open is the key to en-larging a small room. Use light colors and bright, open, widely spaced patterns in the wallcover-ings. Reflective silver wallcoverings can also help. Choose cool colors, which make the walls recede. Smooth textures in the room will also help by reflecting more light. Keep contrasts to a minimum.

☐ Large room: Warm colors will tend to bring the walls of a large room in and make it seem smaller. Dark tones will give the room weight and sub-stance, and tend to bring the room in. Rough tex-tures in the walls, wallcoverings, and other objects all absorb light and will also help, as will contrasting colors.

☐ Cool room: A kitchen on the north side of the

Fig. 13-2. A modified Spanish motif, with dark beams against a white ceiling, arched window, and linoleum in a rich ce-ramic tile pattern (Courtesy of Kitchen Kompact).

house may have a cool feeling to it that you'd like to overcome. Bright, warm colors can liven up a cool room—reds, yellows, and oranges all work well. Remember that warm colors also bring a room in, so if the room is already small, stay to light tones.

☐ Warm room: A kitchen facing west may become overly warm in the afternoon, and has the opposite problems from the cool room. In this case, the obvious solution is to use cool colors in your paint and wallpaper. These cool colors would be colors in the blue, green, and violet range, along with white and silver. Just as the warm colors bring a room in, cool colors move it out, so if the room is already large, you might need a fairly bold shade of color.

☐ Architectural problems: If there are architectural peculiarities in the room, different colors will highlight them and make them stand out. Use the same color throughout the area to help conceal the problem.

WALLCOVERINGS

Paint and wallpaper are the traditional choices in the kitchen, and the choices seem to get wider all the time. Every conceivable shade of paint is available through custom mixing, and there are thousands of wallpapers to compliment or contrast with the paint colors.

Paint

Semigloss paint is the best choice for use in the kitchen. The additives in paint that give it its gloss also control its hardness and durability. Semigloss paint is tougher than flat paint for that reason, and

Fig. 13-3. The casual country look, with white plastered walls, hardwood strip flooring, and lots of collectibles on display (Courtesy of Kitchen Kompact).

142

will withstand grease, steam, and repeated washing much better. Also, its sheen adds a nice, bright finish in the kitchen.

Gloss paint is an even better choice from an upkeep and maintenance standpoint, but because of its high reflectance, it is usually too bright for the kitchen. If your color scheme calls for bright, bold colors, however, gloss paint may work well on the woodwork. Here, brightness and easy care can be nicely combined.

Paint is one area where you shouldn't skimp on quality. A bargain paint is usually thin, with poor hiding power, and may require additional coats to get the same quality of finish you can have with one coat of quality paint.

Price is often a good indicator of a paint's quality. You will find that most of the major brands are priced competitively, and that any one of them will give you a good paint job. Most dealers will let you return what you've bought, including a partial gallon, if you tried it and were totally dissatisfied.

Latex resin paints, which are water based, are the most popular type today. They are easy to work with, need no thinning, and cleanup requires only soap and water. Semi-gloss latex will work fine for most of your wall and ceiling painting needs, but it does not level out as well as the oil based compounds and tends to show brush marks when used on woodwork.

Alkyd resin, an alcohol and acid blend, is the most common of the oil based paints in use today. Alkyd paints are easy to use, level well, and are a very good choice for doors, trim, and other areas where a very smooth finish with no brush marks is desired.

Wallpaper

Wallpaper has become very popular for use in the kitchen in recent years. It is bright, cheerful, and provides a nice change from paint. With the wide range of choices, finding the perfect paper is no problem. You can paper the entire kitchen, the ceiling or one or two walls, or just the soffits.

For best results, choose a washable paper for the kitchen. This type of paper has a durable finish that is resistant to steam and grease, and spills can be easily wiped clean. Avoid flocked and other delicate papers that are unable to withstand the rugged use they'll get in the kitchen.

You can purchase wallpaper dry or prepasted. For most people, the prepasted is the easiest and most convenient to use. A dry adhesive is applied at the factory, and requires only soaking in water to activate it. The paper is cut to length, soaked in a special water tray, then brought to the wall and applied.

Dry paper needs to have adhesive applied on the job site. After cutting to length, the paper is laid out on a table or papering bench, and the adhesive, in the form of a thick liquid, is applied to the paper with a brush or roller. Either type of paper will work fine in the kitchen, and the skills required for hanging either paper can easily be mastered by the do-it-yourselfer.

FLOORING

Flooring choices for the kitchen are equally as wide. There are thousands of colors and patterns available to match with the wallpaper, paint, tile and cabinet colors. There are several different materials available also, many of which are easily installed by the nonprofessional.

☐ Linoleum (Fig. 13-4): Linoleum is the traditional choice for flooring in the kitchen, and it's still popular today. Many of the new, flexible vinyls are very easy to handle and install, and the 12 foot width will cover most kitchens without a seam. Cushioned linoleum is a good choice for withstanding the traffic in the kitchen, and a no-wax finish will keep it looking bright with a minimum of maintenance.

☐ Floor tile: Floor tile in 12-inch squares is probably the easiest of the floorcoverings to install. It goes down quickly with none of the handling problems associated with large rolls of linoleum. Cushioned, no-wax tiles are available from many of the better manufacturers. The only real drawback to tile is the number of seams, which can be dirt collectors.

☐ Ceramic tile: Ceramic tile is a beautiful solution

Fig. 13-4. High-quality, no-wax linoleum is an excellent choice for any kitchen, providing a floor that is durable and easy to clean (Courtesy of Congoleum).

to flooring in the kitchen. There are hundreds of patterns, styles and colors to choose from, installation is not overly difficult, and the floor is so durable it will outlast the kitchen. The drawbacks to ceramic tile are a somewhat higher initial cost, and a feeling of hardness when standing on it for long periods.

☐ Carpet: Kitchen carpeting has become very popular in recent years. Color and pattern choices are good, and the installation can be handled by most do-it-yourselfers. Also, kitchen carpeting is cushioned to have resiliency underfoot. Some types are prone to burning if anything is splattered on them, and traffic patterns tend to show up quickly in a room as heavily used as the kitchen.

☐ Hardwood floor: Hardwood flooring of oak or maple is another elegant choice in the kitchen. The rich, warm wood tones compliment any decor, and today's more durable finishes will stand up to kitchen use with reasonable care. Hardwood flooring can be purchased as traditional strip flooring, which usually requires professional installation, or interlocking, parquet-style blocks, an easier do-it-yourself installation. Hardwood makes a beautiful, durable floor. A relatively high initial cost and a little more maintenance work are its only real drawbacks.

Chapter 14

Active Accessories

WHETHER YOUR KITCHEN HAS BEEN REMODELED from top to bottom or just had a minor facelift, it can benefit from the wide variety of convenient, work- and space-saving kitchen accessories that are now on the market. Manufacturers of kitchen equipment have paid particular interest to the field of add-on accessories in recent years, resulting in a number of kitchen storage and convenience accessories that are inexpensive, easy to install, and can help you maximize what space you have.

Perhaps the most popular of all the kitchen add-ons is the roll-out shelf (Fig. 14-1). Actually shallow drawers, they are installed on tracks in the base cabinets and pull out to allow easier access to the cabinet's contents. A variety of sizes are available, either as all-wood drawers or as bins made of plastic coated wire.

Specialized roll-out units are designed for holding pan lids in an accessible, organized manner (Fig. 14-2). Another unit holds under-the-sink cleaning supplies (Fig. 14-3), and yet another holds the kitchen garbage can (Fig. 14-4).

You can purchase the drawers ready made, or you can build your own to fit the cabinet space you have. A simple box with a dadoed-in bottom is all you need, and you can then purchase the drawer runners by themselves for installation. Roll-out shelves like these are so useful, you'll probably end up installing them in all your cabinets.

One of the most inconvenient storage spots in the entire kitchen is the blind corner cabinet. Used in the corner where two runs of cabinets meet, one cabinet disappears behind the other, creating an almost inaccessible hole that's suitable only for seldom used items.

That space can quickly be made usable with the addition of a device called a blind corner shelf (Fig. 14-5). Attached to the corner cabinet stile near the door hinge, it is merely a half-circular shelf on a pivot. As the door is opened, the shelf rotates out with it, providing access to everything in the cabinet. Some units also feature a slide on the underside of the shelf which allows it to be pulled out of the cabinet an additional 11 inches after opening.

If your kitchen contains a pantry cabinet, or even a broom closet, that space can be effectively put to work with a set of rotating pantry shelves matched with adjustable door bins (Fig. 14-6). The shelves rotate around a central pole, which is easily attached to the top and bottom of the cabinet. The bins, mounted on shelf standards which are attached to the cabinet doors, add additional storage for small,

Fig. 14-1. Roll-out shelves are the height of convenience in the kitchen, making every inch of the cabinets easily accessible (Courtesy of Amerock Corporation).

hard to store items then tend to get lost in the back of the pantry.

One manufacturer of kitchen accessories, Amerock, offers a system for converting your entire pantry cabinet into roll-out shelves (Fig. 14-7). Steel channels mount on the insides of the cabinets, and rollers snap into the channels. A variety of wire or wooden shelves then snap over the rollers, so you can customize the space any way you wish.

Another pantry space saver is the pull-out basket system (Fig. 14-8). This system utilizes a simple frame on a top and bottom roll-out bracket. The frame has a series of hooks on it. Plastic coated wire

baskets of various sizes hang from the hooks. Baskets are available in a variety of depths. Special purpose baskets can be purchased for holding cookbooks, paper towels, trays or bags, spice bottles, and dishtowels. A smaller version of the tray system fits in standard base cabinets. Again, you can customize the storage baskets to fit your space and storage requirements.

A variation on the rotating pantry shelves is the cabinet turntable (Fig. 14-9), also known as the lazy Susan, which can be purchased in a number of sizes for various upper or lower cabinets. A single pole mounts inside the cabinet, and two solid or wire

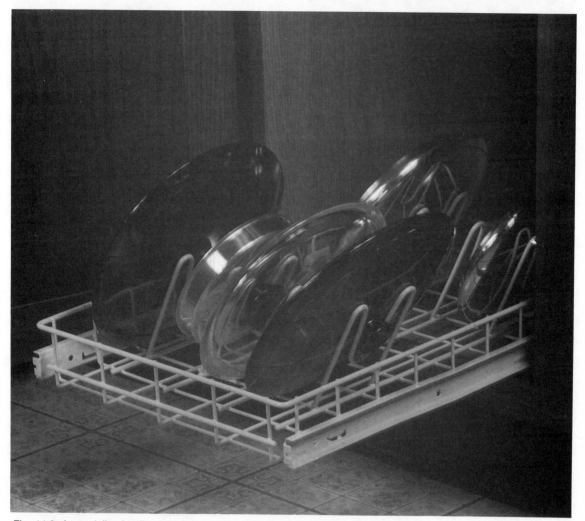

Fig. 14-2. A specialized pull-out rack for pot lids (Courtesy of Amerock Corporation).

mesh trays are attached to the pole. They work wonders for organizing canned goods, spices, (Fig. 14-10), and other items. Door bins (Fig. 14-11), like those for the pantry, are also great for creating additional storage on the backs of cabinet doors.

Air-tight containers are another space saver for storing macaroni, popcorn, and other bulky bagged goods (Fig. 14-12). The containers fit into a rack which is attached to the underside of a shelf, and work well in pantries or any upper cabinet.

A fairly recent trend in maximizing kitchen space

is to use the underside of the upper cabinets. This otherwise unused area can easily be put into service for a variety of uses, creating extra storage while uncluttering your countertops.

A whole range of appliances are now available for undercabinet use, including coffee pots, can openers (Fig. 14-13), toaster ovens, mixers, radios, even a portable TV! The appliances are easy to install, with a simple track mounting system that screws to the bottom of the cabinet.

In addition to appliances, you might want to con-

Fig. 14-3. This rack, perfect for under the sink, houses all the common cleaning supplies (Courtesy of Amerock Corporation).

sider these undercabinet helpers: a cookbook holder (Fig. 14-14); a three-tiered spice rack (Fig. 14-15) for holding spice cans; a knife rack (Fig. 14-16), with slots for up to nine of your most often used knives; or a message center (Fig. 14-17), complete with notepad, pencil and calculator storage, and a cork board for posting notes. All of these units fold up

flat against the underside of the cabinet, hanging down just 1¼ inches, and are easily installed with just a few screws.

For easy access to sponges, scouring pads, and other cleaning items, try a false front tray kit (Fig. 14-18). First, remove the false drawer fronts from the cabinet in front of the sink; they're usually held

Fig. 14-4. A convenient pull-out rack for the garbage can (Courtesy of Amerock Corporation).

Fig. 14-5. The perfect solution for blind corner cabinets are these half shelves, which give access to the entire cabinet. The lower shelf also pulls out (Courtesy of Amerock Corporation).

152

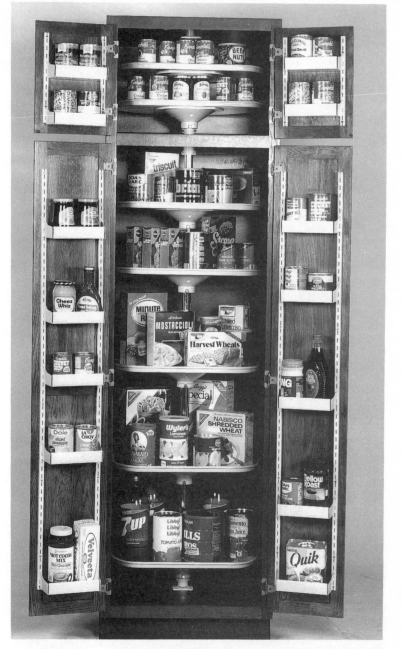

Fig. 14-6. This system, designed to fit a pantry or utility cabinet, features revolving shelves and adjustable door bins. Different sizes and combinations are available to fit different cabinets (Courtesy of Amerock Corporation).

in place with a couple of screws or a small bracket. Install the kit's hinges and trays to the back of the false fronts, then attach the hinges to the cabinet rail. You've easily created some very handy tilt-out storage in an otherwise unused space.

If you have a heavy portable appliance that sees a lot of use, like a mixer or a food processor, spring-loaded brackets are available that fit inside a base cabinet (Fig. 14-19). The brackets, capable of handling loads up to about 30 pounds, allow the appliance to swing up and lock into position for use, then disappear into the cabinet when you're done.

Fig. 14-7. The metal channels of this system screw to the insides of the cabinet, then solid or open bins can be added as desired (Courtesy of Amerock Corporation).

154

Fig. 14-8. The center rack of this system pulls out on a track, and offers adjustable bins of various sizes (Courtesy of Amerock Corporation).

Fig. 14-9. A lazy Susan is another handy way of maximizing the space in a corner cabinet (Courtesy of Amerock Corporation).

Fig. 14-10. Smaller lazy-Susan turntables are available for the upper cabinets, simplifying storage of spices and other small items (Courtesy of Amerock Corporation).

Fig. 14-11. Door bins provide extra storage space on the back of the cabinet doors (Courtesy of Amerock Corporation).

Fig. 14-12. Airtight storage containers in a door-mounted rack simplify the storage of many types of bulk foods (Courtesy of Amerock Corporation).

Fig. 14-13. An under-cabinet can opener. Appliances such as these can free up a lot of otherwise cluttered counter space.

Fig. 14-14. A fold-down cookbook holder offers convenience without utilizing any counter space (Courtesy of Amerock Corporation).

Fig. 14-15. A fold-down, under-cabinet storage rack for spices (Courtesy of Amerock Corporation).

Fig. 14-16. A fold-down knife rack eliminates the need for countertop storage (Courtesy of Amerock Corporation).

Fig. 14-17. For the small kitchen, this message center offered a convenient spot for grocery list, messages, notes and more (Courtesy of Amerock Corporation).

Fig. 14-18. These bins make use of the otherwise wasted space behind the false fronts in a sink base cabinet. The kit comes complete with bins and hinges (Courtesy of Amerock Corporation).

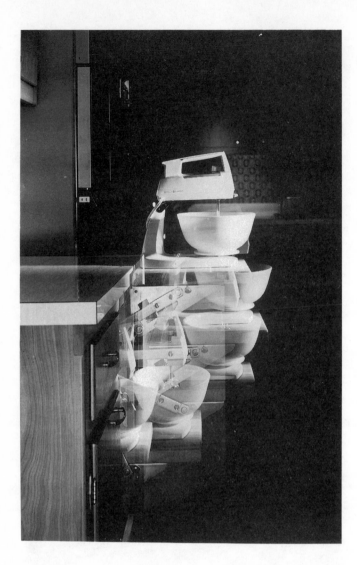

Fig. 14-19. For heavy appliances, a swing-out shelf such as this one is a real labor saver. The appliance sits permanently on the shelf, and is swung up out of the lower cabinet whenever it's needed (Courtesy of Amerock Corporation).

Chapter 15

Cabinet Refacing

WHEN YOU CONSIDER THE OPTIONS OPEN TO YOU for remodeling your kitchen, there doesn't seem to be any middle ground—you either tear everything out and start fresh with new cabinets, or you settle for relatively minor redecorating with new paint and wallpaper. Now there is a middle ground between redecorating and major remodeling: cabinet refacing.

Cabinet refacing is a relative newcomer on the kitchen remodeling scene. The techniques have been around for years, but only recently has this money-saving option gained widespread acceptance. More and more remodeling contractors are offering refacing to their customers, and several companies have sprung up all over the country that specialize in this interesting and often dramatic makeover procedure. In fact, many homeowners are undertaking cabinet refacing as a do-it-yourself project, and with very good results.

The refacing process is really quite simple, although the actual work requires time and patience for good results. The existing cabinet doors and drawer fronts are removed, the existing cabinets are refaced with wood or plastic laminates, and new doors and drawer fronts are installed. Many people choose to install new counters and update old appliances at the same time, but even with that, a carefully scheduled job can be done in just a few days.

THE PROS AND CONS OF CABINET REFACING

Cabinet refacing has some very definite advantages and disadvantages. They must be analyzed and weighed carefully before you make a decision for or against the procedure.

The biggest advantage side for most people is money. They really don't want or need new cabinets but their kitchen is drab and outdated, and simple redecorating is not enough of an improvement. With cabinet refacing, they can achieve a whole new look in the kitchen that closely approximates new cabinets, but for a fraction of the cost. Where all new cabinets for an average-sized kitchen might run around $4,000 installed, the existing cabinets can be refaced and new doors and drawer fronts added for about $1,500. That $2,500 difference can go a long way toward paying for new appliances!

Another advantage is time. A complete kitchen remodeling can often take 3 weeks or more, and during most of that time, you are left without kitchen facilities. Refacing, on the other hand, doesn't usually begin until the new doors and drawer fronts have been fabricated. Tear-out is minimal, and even with new appliances, counters, and flooring, a complete kitchen make-over can be done in as little as 5 days—and you'll still have the use of your kitchen for most of that time.

Note that cabinet refacing is not a cheap-looking quick fix for a tired kitchen. A number of high quality solid woods and laminates can be used, and the new doors and drawer fronts are the same as those used on new cabinets. The end result of a refacing job that's been done by a skilled contractor or a competent and patient do-it-yourselfer is quite dramatic. In fact, many refaced kitchens are indistinguishable from kitchens with all new cabinets. It takes close scrutiny and a knowledge of what to look for to tell the two apart.

The refacing job also can be combined with some minor cabinet modifications that can make a big difference in how efficient the kitchen is to work in. Roll-out shelves can be added, under-cabinet accessories or even under-cabinet lighting is possible, and you can even add a new pantry cabinet in an unused corner that is built to match the refaced cabinets. Take a look at the selection of accessories in Chapter 14 to get some ideas.

Although there are some very definite advantages to cabinet refacing, there is a very definite down side also—lack of design flexibility. With refacing, the cabinet layout you have now is what you'll still be left with when the job is done. Minor changes can be made—a larger or smaller opening in a cabinet to accommodate a new oven, for example—but space cannot be reapportioned within the room.

Larger countertop runs aren't possible, changes or updates in electrical wiring are difficult, and modifying the plumbing or relocating the appliances is just about impossible. In short, if you don't like the layout of the kitchen as it is now, or if you're seriously lacking storage space or countertop area, refacing is not for you.

Refacing is also not intended as a repair procedure for deteriorating cabinets. Broken doors will obviously be taken care of and sticking drawers can usually be repaired, but a successful refacing procedure depends to a large extent on the condition of the existing faceframes and cabinet cases. Also, refacing does nothing for the cabinet's interior.

MATERIALS

Solid wood and plastic laminates are two materials used in cabinet refacing. The choice is dependent on the look you're trying to achieve in the kitchen and, to a lesser degree, the type of materials used elsewhere in the house, particularly in rooms adjacent to the kitchen. Some cabinet refacing companies specialize in only one material or the other. Be sure to ask first which material they carry when selecting a contractor.

Solid Wood

If you choose to use wood as the refacing material, there are several options. Some contractors use ¼-inch-thick material, others use ⅛ inch, and still others use the paper-thin veneers that are commonly used in furniture construction. There are advantages and disadvantages to each. The thicker materials are easier to work with, especially for the do-it-yourselfer, but the thin veneers often produce seams that are easier to conceal.

Many larger lumberyards carry door skin material, which is ideal for cabinet refacing. You also can use ¼-inch lumber-core plywood with good results. For veneers or exotic woods, you'll probably be looking at a special order.

For the doors and drawer fronts, solid lumber is used. Choices of style are just as wide open as they are with new cabinets; you can choose from slab doors, flat panel doors, raised panel doors, etc.

You'll also have a wide variety of wood types to choose from. Oak is very popular, as is birch. Other wood species, often prohibitively expensive when used to build entire cabinets, might now be worth considering. Cherry, black walnut, and even more exotic woods are all possibilities.

Plastic Laminates

With the rise in popularity of the European-look in frameless cabinetry, the use of plastic laminates as a refacing material has also risen. Laminates offer a tremendous variety of colors and patterns, and in many ways may prove easier for the do-it-yourselfer to install.

Doors and drawer fronts are usually constructed from plywood or particleboard, then faced with matching laminates. Flat slab doors are the usual choice, and the concealed hinges that are an important part of the frameless look can easily be adapted to the new doors and existing cases.

THE REFACING PROCEDURE

The cabinet refacing process can be broken down into three basic steps. First, the existing cabinet doors and drawer fronts are removed and discarded. The old cabinets are then repaired if necessary, cleaned, and refaced with new material. The final step is the installation of new doors, drawer fronts, and matching trim. In the case of wood refacing, there is also a fourth step: staining and lacquering.

Removing the Old Doors and Drawer Fronts

Removing the old doors (Fig. 15-1), is no more involved then unscrewing the hinges from the cabinets. Discard the doors and, unless they're in very good condition, discard the hinges also. Remove and discard magnetic or roller catches that were used with the old doors.

Most drawer fronts are held in place with a combination of glue and nails. To remove the fronts, first remove the handles or knobs—they are usually screwed in from the back and also help hold the drawer front in place. Carefully work a thin, stiff putty knife in between the drawer and the drawer front to create a gap, then use a stout screwdriver (Figs. 15-2 & 15-3), or other tool to pry off the drawer front. Carefully remove any nails that remain protruding through the drawer (Fig. 15-4). Discard the old drawer fronts.

If the drawer fronts are an integral part of the whole drawer assembly, you'll need to adapt this

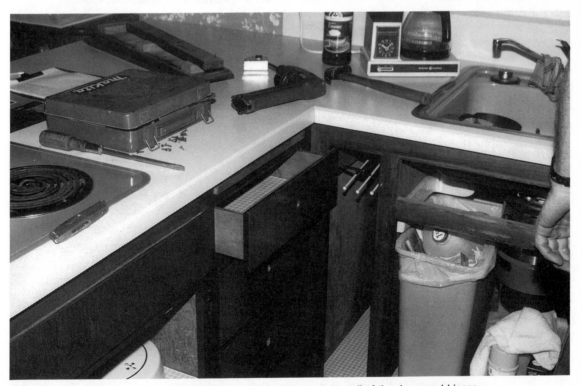

Fig. 15-1. The first step in the cabinet refacing procedure is to remove all of the doors and hinges.

Fig. 15-2. Use a heavy screwdriver or similar tool to pry off the old drawer fronts.

Fig. 15-3. Also remove and discard false panels, such as this one in front of the sink.

Fig. 15-4. When the drawer fronts have been removed, remove all protruding nails from the drawer assembly, which remains in place and will be reused.

procedure to what's existing. For example, you might need to disassemble all or part of the existing drawer, then make new fronts that are slotted or dovetailed like the old ones. In some cases, entirely new drawers may be needed.

Preparing the Old Cabinets

If there are any repairs needed on the existing cabinet cases or faceframes, do those first. Minor alterations are possible, as in the case of the new oven mentioned above, and those should be done next. For example, the faceframe could be trimmed to accommodate a larger appliance, or fillers could be added to close the opening down to fit a smaller unit.

It will probably be necessary to remove some of the appliances (Fig. 15-5), particularly range hoods, built-in ovens, and built-in microwaves. Study the cabinets and visualize applying the facings. It will quickly become apparent which appliances are in the way and will need to be removed. Refer to Chapter 7 for instructions on safe appliance removal.

Wash the cabinets with a solution of TSP and water to remove grease deposits, just as you would to prepare a wall for painting. If the cabinet is painted with gloss or semigloss paint, or if it's finished with a smooth glossy lacquer or other coating, prepare it for the new facing by sanding the outside surfaces with fine sandpaper. Sanding will roughen the surface and remove the gloss. Be careful not to round the corners over.

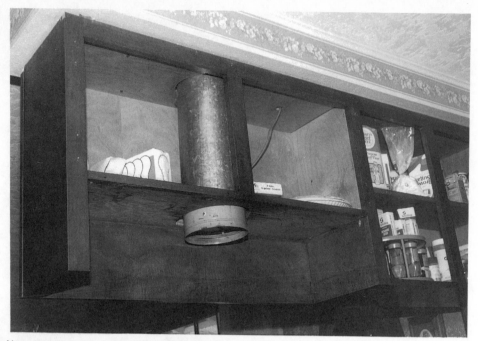

Fig. 15-5. Also remove any appliances that will be in the way of the refacing, such as the range hood.

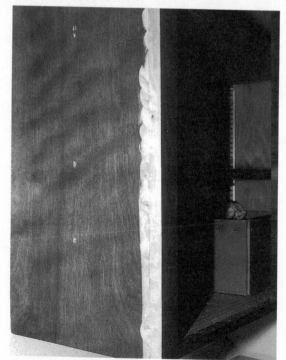

Fig. 15-6. Use a disk sander to remove an area where the faceframe overhung the side of the cabinet.

If the old cabinets have faceframes that extend over the sides of the cabinets, these overhanging edges will need to be removed to ensure a smooth fit with the new facing (Figs. 15-6 & 15-7). Depending on how large the overhang is, you can remove it with a belt or disk sander, a wood rasp, or a router.

APPLYING WOOD FACING

Wood facing can be applied in one of two ways. Large sheets of material can be placed over the entire cabinet face and the openings routed out. This is the fastest and easiest method, but it results in a facing with all the grain running in the same direction. If you look closely at the existing cabinet, you will see that the sides have vertical grain and the faceframes, as a result of how they're constructed, have both vertical and horizontal grain.

The preferred method, which is more time consuming but which results in a much more realistic and attractive cabinet, is to face the case and faceframe with individual pieces. The grain then can be oriented to match and duplicate the appearance of a new, solid wood cabinet.

Apply solid pieces to the sides of the cabinets first (Fig. 15-8). Carefully measure and cut the facing material to size, then hold it in place to check the fit. Scribe and trim the piece as needed to get an exact fit. If desired, cover some seams, such as those against the wall or against the ceiling, with molding so they do not have to fit precisely (Fig. 15-9).

Coat the back of the piece with a good grade of waterproof woodworking glue (Fig. 15-10), fit it to the cabinet, and secure it with small brads (Fig. 15-11). Try to keep the brads confined to areas that will be covered with trim. When all of the sides are done, cover any exposed upper cabinet bottoms with facing also (Fig. 15-12).

Apply the faceframe pieces next. Measure the width of the existing frame pieces, and rip the facing material slightly wider than that on a table saw equipped with a fine-toothed plywood blade. If you are using thin veneers, use whatever cutting method is recommended by your dealer.

Apply the faceframe strips with glue, using brads sparingly. Use the construction of the existing faceframe as a guide, and apply the facing in the same manner, using butt joints where the horizontal and vertical strips meet (Fig. 15-13 & Fig. 15-14). Carefully align the strip edges with the outside corners of the cabinets, and let the excess hang over to the inside.

After all the strips have been applied and the

Fig. 15-7. Carefully sand off any slight protrusions where two cabinets meet.

Fig. 15-8. Apply new wood panels, in this case fabricated from ¼-inch oak doors skin material, to the cabinet sides.

Fig. 15-9. You can use new, matching oak trim to conceal irregular areas at the ceiling and wall.

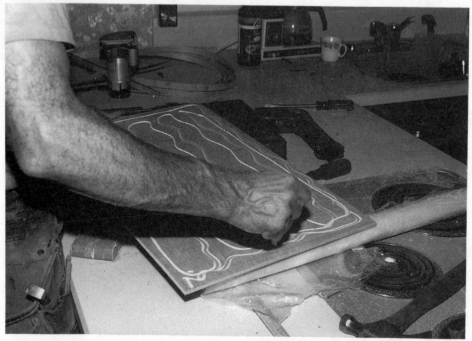

Fig. 15-10. Apply a liberal coating of waterproof woodworking glue to the back of the panel.

Fig. 15-11. Use small brads—in this case they are being applied with an air gun—mainly around the edges to secure the panel while the glue sets.

Fig. 15-12. If the undersides of the wall cabinets will be exposed, face them also.

Fig. 15-13. Apply faceframe strips both horizontally and vertically to duplicate the look of the original faceframe.

Fig. 15-14. Use simple butt joints where the strips join, again duplicating the look of the original faceframe.

glue has been allowed sufficient time to set, use a router equipped with straight (not beveled) trimming bit, and trim the strips flush with the inside edges of the existing faceframe. This will result in a small rounded area in each corner (Fig. 15-15), which can be left as is or squared off with a small wood file.

If you are using thin veneers, the joint between the facing on the faceframe and the facing on the cabinet sides will be virtually invisible. This saves you additional work, but does not match the actual appearance of a new wood cabinet.

To duplicate this look and also to conceal the joint left by thicker facing materials, use ¾-inch facing veneer (Fig. 15-16). This material, commonly used for finishing off the front edge of plywood shelves, is sold by the roll at most lumber yards in a variety of wood types. Apply it full width to the front edge of the cabinet's side with glue, and it will conceal the joint in the facing while closely approximating the realistic look of the edge of a solid wood faceframe.

APPLYING PLASTIC LAMINATE FAC

One of the appeals of new plastic laminate-faced nets is the smooth, sleek appearance which is most completely devoid of any seams. This look ca be closely approximated with laminate facing, and without the close fitting work and grain direction problems associated with wood facings.

Laminates are applied with contact cement, which is easy to use but requires careful fitting and installation. After trimming and dry fitting each piece, the contact cement is applied to both the cabinet face and the back side of the laminate panel. Carefully place one edge of the piece in the exact location without allowing the rest of the panel to contact the cabinet. When it's perfectly aligned, press the rest of the panel against the cabinet. The piece will adhere immediately, with no room for adjustment, so make your alignments carefully.

After sanding and preparing cabinets as outlined above, laminate pieces are cut to fit the undersides of the wall cabinets. Carefully measure, cut, and

Fig. 15-15. Routing results in a small rounded area at each corner. The area is barely noticable, but can easily be removed with a file if desired.

clean fit, then apply them with

counters with full backsplashes
apply the laminate backsplash to the
en the backsplash is complete, install
counters or reface and reinstall the exist-
unter.

Laminate pieces are applied to the sides of the cabinets next. Again, carefully fit and scribe them in place before gluing. Trim is not normally used with this type of cabinet, so fits should be exact.

Last, apply the face laminate. Unlike wood facing, laminate facing is applied in one large piece, which results in it's seamless appearance. Cut the face piece so it covers as much of one run as possible, then secure it with a double coat of contact cement. Use a router with a laminate trimming bit to cut the door openings, following the inside edge of the faceframe as a guide.

NEW DOORS AND DRAWER FRONTS

New doors and drawer fronts are usually made up in advance, so the job is not delayed while you wait for them. If desired, you can make your own doors, or you can leave this specialized task to a cabinet shop and just do your own refacing.

Wooden doors (Fig. 15-17) are usually made up to match the sizes of the original doors, as are the drawer fronts (Fig. 15-18). Laminate doors, on the other hand, are often made larger than the originals so that they cover more of the cabinet's face and more closely approximate the look of new, frameless cabinetry.

Install the doors with new exposed (Fig. 15-19) or concealed hinges, whichever is more visually pleasing to you and compliments the style of the cabinets. Install drawer fronts with glue and then secure them by nailing through the drawer into the back side of the drawer front (Fig. 15-20).

Fig. 15-16. Use veneer strips, which are purchased by the roll, to conceal the joint between the face and the side of the cabinet. Using ¾-inch-wide material gives the appearance of the edge of a solid lumber faceframe.

Fig. 15-17. New doors can be made up in any desired style.

Fig. 15-18. Construct new drawer fronts from solid lumber and finish them to match the cabinets.

Fig. 15-19. The new doors for this installation are mounted with exposed, antique brass hinges.

Fig. 15-20. Attach the new drawer fronts to the old drawer assembly with glue and nails, then install the knobs.

FINISHING OFF THE INSTALLATION

With the installation of the doors, the laminate refacing is complete. With wood, you'll still need to stain the new material. Test stain colors on scraps of facing until you find the right shade, then stain the cabinets following the instructions on the stain can. Take your time, and allow sufficient ventilation.

When the stain is dry, protect the cabinets with a lacquer or polyurethane finish, which can be applied by spray or brush. Follow the manufacturer's instructions carefully.

The final step is to apply wood molding as desired (Fig. 15-21), which has been prestained to match the new cabinets. If desired, you can also redo the counters with ceramic tile or new laminates, then trim them off with matching wood (Fig. 15-22). Another nice touch is to install new window sills of matching wood or laminate (Fig. 15-23).

Fig. 15-21. No detail should be overlooked when refacing. In this case, the old supports for the eating counter overhang were removed and replaced with new ones cut from solid oak lumber.

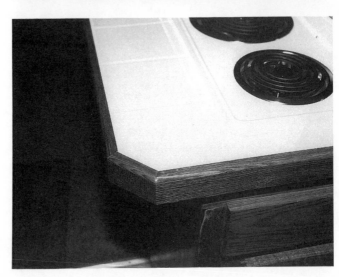

Fig. 15-22. New ceramic tile was applied directly over the old plastic laminate countertop, then finished off with oak strips along the edges that match the new cabinet facings.

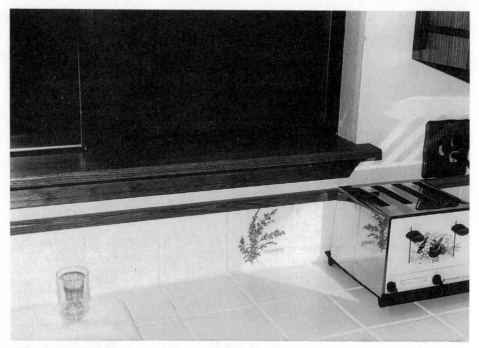

Fig. 15-23. Other nice details that mark a quality installation include a new oak stool and apron for the window, and oak molding to trim off the top of the counters.

Appendix

Appendix

Sources

For more information on some of the products and services available to help you remodel your kitchen, you can write to the following addresses:

American Home Lighting Institute
435 N. Michigan Ave.
Chicago, IL 60611

American Olean Tile Company
1000 Cannon Ave.
P.O. Box 271
Lansdale, PA 19446-0271

American Plywood Association
P.O. Box 11700
Tacoma, WA 98411

American Standard
3 Crossroads of Commerce, Ste. 100
Rolling Meadows, IL 60008
(Kitchen and bath fixtures)

Amerock Corporation
P.O. Box 7018
Rockford, IL 61125-7018
(Kitchen accessories)

Congoleum Corporation
Resilient Flooring Division
195 Belgrove Dr.
Kearny, NJ 07032

Diamond Cabinets
P.O. Box 547
Hillsboro, OR 97123

E.I. du Pont de Nemours Company, Inc.
Corian Building Products
Wilmington, DE 19898

Kitchen Concepts
447 NE Greenwood
Bend, OR 97701
(Kitchen design)

Kitchen Kompact, Inc. (Cabinets)
KK Plaza
P.O. Box 868
Jeffersonville, IN 47131

Lightolier
100 Lighting Way
Secaucus, NJ 07094
(Lighting products)

Medallion Kitchens of Minnesota
180 Industrial Blvd.
Waconia, MN 55387
(Cabinets)

Merillat Industries, Inc.
2072 West Beecher Rd.
Adrian, MI 49221
(Cabinets)

Merrit Industries
12185 - 86th Ave.
Surrey, British Columbia, Canada V3W 3H8
(Cabinets)

Moen, A Division of Stanadyne
377 Woodland Ave.
Elyria, OH 44036-2111
(Faucets)

Nutone Products
Madison & Red Bank Rds.
Cincinnati, OH 45227
(Kitchen and bath products)

Scheirich Cabinetry
P.O. Box 37120
Louisville, KY 40233-7120

Wallcovering Information Bureau
66 Morris Ave.
Springfield, NJ 07081

Western Wood Products Association
522 SW Fifth Ave.
Portland, OR 97204-2122

Wood Moulding and Millwork Producers
P.O. Box 25278
Portland, OR 97225

Wilsonart Laminates
600 General Bruce Dr.
Temple, TX 76501
(Plastic laminates)

Index

Index

Other Bestsellers From TAB

☐ **MASTER HOUSEHOLD ELECTRICAL WIRING—2nd Edition—James L. Kittle**

Update dangerously old wiring in your house. Add an outdoor, dusk-to-dawn light. Repair a malfunctioning thermostat and add an automatic setback. You can do all this and more—easily and safely—for much less than the cost of having a professional do it for you! You can remodel, expand, and modernize existing wiring correctly and safely with this practical guide to household wiring. From testing to troubleshooting, you can do it all yourself. Add dimmer switches and new outlets . . . ground your TV or washer . . . make simple appliances repair . . . set up outside wiring . . . put in new fixtures and more! 304 pp., 273 illus.

Paper $18.95   **Hard $24.95**
Book No. 2987

☐ **SUNSPACES—HOME ADDITIONS FOR YEAR-ROUND NATURAL LIVING—John Mauldin, Photography by John H. Mauldin and Juan L. Espinosa**

Have you been thinking of enclosing your porch to increase your living space? Want to add a family room, but want the best use of the space for the money? Do you want information on solar energy and ideas on how you can make it work in your home? If "yes" is your answer to any of these questions, you'll want to own this fascinating guide! 256 pp., 179 illus.

Paper $17.95   **Hard $21.95**
Book No. 2816

☐ **HOME PLUMBING MADE EASY: AN ILLUSTRATED MANUAL—James L. Kittle**

Here, in one heavily illustrated, easy-to-follow volume, is all the how-to-do-it information needed to perform almost any home plumbing job, including both water and waste disposal systems. And what makes this guide superior to so many other plumbing books is the fact that there's plenty of hands-on instruction, meaningful advice, practical safety tips, and emphasis on getting the job done as easily and professionally as possible! 272 pp., 250 illus.

Paper $12.95   **Hard $14.95**
Book No. 2797

☐ **TILE FLOORS—INSTALLING, MAINTAINING AND REPAIRING—Dan Ramsey**

Now you can easily install resilient or traditional hard tiles on both walls and floors. Find out how to buy quality resilient floor products at reasonable cost . . . and examine the types and sizes of hard tiles available. Get step-by-step instructions for laying out the floor, selecting needed tools, and adhesives, cutting tile, applying adhesives, and more. 192 pp., 200 illus. 4 pages in full color

Paper $17.95   **Hard $22.95**
Book No. 1998

☐ **101 KITCHEN PROJECTS FOR THE WOODWORKER—Percy W. Blandford**

These 101 practical as well as decorative projects for every level of woodworking ability are sure to provide pleasure and satisfaction for builder and cook alike! Included are bread and cheese boards, carving boards and butcher blocks, trays, cookbook stand and stacking vegetable bin, spatulas, forks, spring tongs, mug racks, pivoting and parallel towel rails, spice racks, tables, a hutch, and much, much more! 270 pp., 214 illus.

Paper $17.95   **Hard $23.95**
Book No. 2884

☐ **ADD A ROOM: A PRACTICAL GUIDE TO EXPANDING YOUR HOME—Paul Bianchina**

Overflowing with helpful diagrams, photographs, and illustrations, this indispensable guide focuses on the professional details that make the difference between a room addition that blends in and one that looks like an afterthought. It's far more than a volume of plans or architectural ideas . . . it's a complete how-to-do-it manual that leaves no question unanswered. The types of rooms you can build using this guide include a garage, a room on top of your garage, a sunspace or greenhouse, a family or rec room, a bathroom, and many others. 400 pp., 360 illus.

Paper $19.95   **Hard $27.95**
Book No. 2811

☐ **THE ILLUSTRATED DICTIONARY OF BUILDING MATERIALS AND TECHNIQUES—Paul Bianchina**

Here's a one-stop reference for do-it-yourselfers and professionals that gives you clear, straightforward definitions for all of the tools, terms, materials, and techniques used by builders, contractors, architects, and other building professionals. It includes almost 4,000 terms and abbreviations from the simple to the complex, from slang to the latest technical information. 272 pp., 172 illus.

Paper $18.95   **Hard $22.95**
Book No. 2681

☐ **HOW TO BE YOUR OWN ARCHITECT—2nd Edition—Murray C. Goddard and Mike and Ruth Wolverton**

This revision version of a long-time bestseller gives you all the expert assistance needed to design your own dream house like a professional. You'll save the money that most custom-home builders put out in architects' fees—an estimated 12% to 15% of the total construction costs—to pay for more of these extras you'd like. 288 pp., 369 illus.

Paper $12.95   **Hard $14.95**
Book No. 1790

Other Bestsellers From TAB

☐ **HARDWOOD FLOORS—INSTALLING, MAINTAIN-
ING, AND REPAIRING—Dan Ramsey**

This comprehensive guide includes all the guidance you
need to install, restore, maintain, or repair all types of hardwood flooring at costs far below those charged by professional builders and maintenance services. From details on
how to select the type of wood floors best suited to your
home, to time- and money-saving ways to keep floors in top
condition. 160 pp., 230 illus. 4 pages in full color
Paper $14.95   **Hard $18.95**
Book No. 1928

☐ **DO YOUR OWN DRYWALL—An Illustrated Guide—
Arnold Kozloski**

Proper installation of interior plasterboard or drywall
is a must-have skill for successful home building or remodeling. Now, there's a new time- and money-saving alternative:
this excellent step-by-step guide to achieving professional-
quality drywalling results, the first time and every time! Even
joint finishing, the drywalling step that is most dreaded by
do-it-yourselfers, can be a snap when you know what you're
doing. 160 pp., 161 illus.
Paper $9.95   **Hard $10.95**
Book No. 1838

☐ **WHAT'S IT WORTH?—A HOME INSPECTION AND
APPRAISAL MANUAL—Joseph Scaduto**

Here's a guide that can save home buyers thousands
of dollars in unexpected maintenance and repair costs! You'll
find out what types of structural problems occur in older and
in new homes, even condominiums . . . cover everything
from foundations and crawl spaces to attics and roofs . . .
and learn simple ''tricks of the trade''! 256 pp., 281 illus.
Paper $10.95   **Hard $12.95**
Book No. 1761

☐ **EFFECTIVE LIGHTING FOR HOME AND
BUSINESS—Dan Ramsey**

Now this completely up-to-date sourcebook provides all
the information you need to update the lighting in your home
or business . . . indoors *and* outdoors! Find all the most modern lighting theories, wiring and fixture information, and installation techniques given in easy-to-follow, step-by-step
format. Plus there are 16 complete lighting plans! 224 pp.,
380 illus.
Paper $11.95   **Hard $13.50**
Book No. 1658

**Send $1 for the new TAB Catalog describing over 1300 titles currently in print and receive
a coupon worth $1 off on your next purchase from TAB.**

*Prices subject to change without notice.

To purchase these or any other books from TAB, visit your local bookstore, return this coupon, or call
toll-free 1-800-233-1128 (In PA and AK call 1-717-794-2191).

Product No.	Hard or Paper	Title	Quantity	Price

☐ Check or money order enclosed made payable to TAB BOOKS Inc.

Charge my   ☐ VISA   ☐ MasterCard   ☐ American Express

Acct. No. _____ Exp. _____

Signature _____

Please Print
Name _____

Company _____

Address _____

City _____

State _____ Zip _____

Subtotal	
Postage/Handling ($5.00 outside U.S.A. and Canada)	$2.50
In PA add 6% sales tax	
TOTAL	

Mail coupon to:

TAB BOOKS Inc.
Blue Ridge Summit
PA 17294-0840   BC